The
 GPAMaxx
Guide to

D0226301

ACING
THE PUBLIC
UNIVERSITY

Jeff Gimpel

Published by GPAMaxx LLC, Boulder, Colorado
www.GPAMaxx.com

Publisher's Cataloging-in-Publication (Provided by Quality Books, Inc.)
Gimpel, Jeff.
    The GPAMaxx guide to acing the public university /
Jeff Gimpel. — First edition.
    pages cm
    Includes index.
    LCCN 2015902929
    ISBN 978-0-9915357-0-5 (pbk)
    ISBN 978-0-9915357-1-2 (ebk)

    1. College student orientation. 2. Study skills.
3. Public universities and colleges. I. Title.
II. Title: GPA Maxx guide to acing the public university.

LB2343.3.G557 2015   378.1'98
                QBI15-600065

Printed in the United States of America
First Edition

10 9 8 7 6 5 4 3 2 1

For more information about GPAMaxx® and the services that we offer, visit us at www.GPAMaxx.com or call us toll-free at 1-855-GPAMaxx.

Dedication

*For all students planning to attend
a public university*

Contents

Introduction 1
    A Tale of Two Students 1
    Why This Book? 6
    What's in This Book? 9
    Who Is This Book For? 10
    How to Use This Book 12

Part I: Why You Need Your Own College Strategy ... 13

1   The GPAMaxx Strategy: A First Look 15
    The GPAMaxx Strategy: A Brief Overview 18
    The GPAMaxx Cardinal Rules 21

2   Academic Advising: Why You Need to
    Look Out for Yourself 23
    Why You Need to Be Your Own Best Academic Advisor 25
    Working with Your Academic Advisor 28

Part II: Demystifying the Grade Game 29

3   Grades and GPAs: The Basics 31
    Letter Grading 32
    Pass/Fail Grading 33
    University Academic Calendars:
        The Semester vs. the Quarter System 33
    Credit Hours 34
    GPA Explained 36
    Nothing Lasts Forever, but Bad Grades
        Come Awfully Close 39

4   Your College GPA and the Big Picture 45

Your Opportunities On and Off Campus 46

Your Career. 48

Your Graduate School Prospects 49

Other Factors 50

5   Making the Grade: What You Should Know
About University Grading Practices 53

Grading on the Curve 54

Criteria-Based Grading. 56

Weed-Out Courses 58

What the Different Approaches to Grading Mean for You. . . . 59

6   The GPA Goalpost: Graduating with
GPA-Based Honors 61

Why You Need to Know Where Your
University's GPA Goalpost Sits. 62

Graduation with GPA-Based Honors 63

Some Examples 64

Part III: Getting to Know Your University Road Map. . 73

7   Know Your University Road Map—Your Degree Plan:
GPAMaxx Cardinal Rule #1 75

A Sample Degree Plan 76

Students and Their Degree Plans:
Potential Fundamental Blunders 78

A Study in Contrasts: Students Who Know
Their Degree Plan 80

8   Dissecting University Degree Plans. 83

Rules and Policies Governing Degree Plans. 83

Degree Plans Made Easy: Component Coursework 85

General Education Courses. 85

Major and Minor Courses. 90

Elective Courses. 93

Online Coursework 96

Part IV: Two Key Strategies for Acing the Public University. **99**

9   Credit by Examination: An Overview 101

Types of Exams to Earn CBE. 102

10   Making the Most of Credit by Examination 111

Strategic Advantages to Using Credit by Examination. 112

A Pitfall of CBE: Accepting Credit for an Introductory
Class, Then Struggling in the Follow-Up Course. 121

Preparing on Your Own for Exams to Earn
Credit by Examination. 125

Prioritizing Your Use of Credit by Examination. 128

11   Taking Transfer Courses: An Overview 133

Transfer Courses vs. Courses at Your University 133

Taking Transfer Courses in the Same State
Is Usually Straightforward 134

College Courses in High School: Dual Enrollment 135

Strategic Advantages of Taking Transfer Courses 137

Potential Pitfalls of Transfer Coursework 143

Part V: Getting to Know Yourself **149**

12   Know Yourself as a Student:
GPAMaxx Cardinal Rule #2 151

Getting to Know Yourself as a Student: Necessary Steps. . . .153

13   Finding Your Inner Student. 159

Determining Your Academic Strengths and Weaknesses . . .160

Discovering Your Preferred Format:
Your Ideal Instructional and Grading Formats 164

The Best Course for Your GPA Might Be the One
You Don't Take 166

Part VI: Learning to Professor Shop 169

14 Know How to Professor Shop:
GPAMaxx Cardinal Rule #3 171

Knowing How an Instructor Previously Graded
Can Help You 172

Professor Shopping: A Case Study 173

15 Professor Shopping: A Tutorial 175

Steps to Professor Shop 175

Five Tips for Effective Professor Shopping 178

Questions to Ask Yourself Each Time You Professor Shop . .182

Part VII: Applying the GPAMaxx Strategy
on Your Own 183

16 Developing Your University Game Plan
with the GPAMaxx Strategy 185

Why You Need a University Game Plan 186

Who Was the GPAMaxx Game Plan Module
Designed For? 189

Using the GPAMaxx Game Plan Module:
A Primer 190

You and Your University Game Plan:
An Ongoing Relationship 208

17 Selecting Your Courses with the GPAMaxx Strategy 209

Using the GPAMaxx Course Selection Module:
A Primer 210

Analyzing Your Potential Courses Is Time Well Spent 229

Case Studies
The GPAMaxx Course Selection Module in Action 231
    Case Study #1: Selecting Courses for Your General
        Education Requirements. 232
    Case Study #2: Selecting Courses in Your Major 240

Resources. **249**
    Credit by Examination 250
    Transfer Coursework. 250
    State-Supported College Information Websites 255

Endnotes **261**

Index. **265**

About GPAMaxx® **275**

About the Author. **275**

INTRODUCTION

A Tale of Two Students

The following story is based on the experiences of several people we know. It repeats itself countless times across public university campuses every year.

Two classmates from the same high school graduating class, Tyler and Mason, attend State University, a highly regarded public university in their state. Both Tyler and Mason major in business administration, and both are in the fall semester of their fourth year at State University.

In high school, Tyler was a strong student who made almost straight As. He took Advanced Placement (AP) classes, and he even scored high enough on a number of AP exams to qualify for college credit. Back then, his classes came pretty easily to him, and he did well on just about everything—term papers, essay exams, multiple-choice tests, and class projects. He put in a lot of hours on his homework, and experience taught him that if he spent enough time and made the effort, he'd get the high grades he deserved. Like many other kids who ace high school, Tyler assumed that he could whiz through college simply by following his high school playbook.

In contrast, Mason had a mixed high school record. He took several AP classes, but he wasn't an all-around academic all-star. Unlike Tyler, Mason had definite strengths and weaknesses in the classroom. Math and science never came easily to him, and his high school grades reflected that weakness. Mason also did much better on some types of tests and school assignments than on others.

While Tyler did nothing outside of his high school classes to prepare himself for college, Mason took a more strategic approach. He understood that he had distinct academic strengths and weaknesses, and he realized that what he had learned in high school wasn't enough to prepare him for success in college. He knew that State University was full of students who were just as academically talented and hardworking as he was—if not more so. To get good grades at State University, Mason knew, he'd need to do more than just study hard. He'd need a university game plan that maximized his strengths and minimized his weaknesses.

Mason began to develop his university game plan while still in high school. He learned about the course requirements he would need to fulfill to graduate from State University, and the different ways he could do so. He found out which courses he could test out of entirely and still get college credit, through both AP and other exams. This allowed him to earn credit for several of his State University courses before he even finished high school.

He also found out that he could take the required courses in his weakest subjects—math and science—at the local community college. Courses there would count toward his degree, but the grades he earned wouldn't have any impact on his grade point average, or GPA, at State University. This enabled Mason to complete all his math and science college requirements the summer before he started at State University.

Did you know?

More than $\frac{2}{3}$ of all public university students don't graduate on time.[1]

Preparing for exams to test out of college courses while still in high school and taking community college classes after graduation required real discipline and commitment. But Mason's efforts paid big dividends once he got to State University. He arrived with more than a semester's worth of college credit that counted toward his degree.

Tyler and Mason continued to take different approaches at State University. Tyler thought he would major in business administration, but he wasn't absolutely sure. So instead of taking introductory business courses that would fulfill requirements toward a degree in business administration, he focused largely on the basic courses required of all students. He didn't give much thought to finding courses that would be a good fit for him and position him to get high grades. Tyler believed that hard work would give him the edge in any course he took. If he simply put in enough time and effort, he would get the high grades he was used to in high school.

Did you know?

The size of the average student loan debt has ballooned 58% since 2005.[2]

Mason took a different path. Throughout college, he maintained a university game plan. Before registering for his courses, Mason took the time to analyze his course choices. He made sure he selected only classes that satisfied requirements for business majors. Mason also consistently sought out courses that were the best fit for his learning style. When multiple courses fulfilled the same degree requirement, he picked the one that offered him the best odds for getting a high grade. And finally, when more than one instructor taught a class that seemed likely to be a good fit for him, he researched each instructor's grading history and signed up for the one who tended to give higher grades.

Fast-forward three years. Both Tyler and Mason are in the fall semester of their fourth year of college. While each came from the same high school and has the same major, they have had very different experiences at State University.

First, Tyler. Although he earned college credit for a couple of courses by passing AP exams in high school, Tyler won't be graduating on schedule in the spring. He eventually chose to major in business administration, but because he didn't take the required courses for business majors during freshman year, he'll need an extra year to complete his degree. Staying a fifth year at State University will force Tyler to take out more student loans and cause him to lose out on any income he would have earned in a job.

What's worse, even when Tyler does graduate, it's doubtful that he'll have the GPA needed to get one of the more sought-after, high-paying jobs open to graduating seniors, or to get into a reputable graduate school. Freshman year at State University hit Tyler like a freight train. He underestimated how hard it would be to get good grades. Tyler had been a great high school student—but so had most of the other students at State University.

Tyler's low freshman-year grades unfortunately cast a shadow over his entire college experience. He learned firsthand that it's both difficult and time-consuming to raise a low GPA to even an average one. As a result, he's had to forgo a lot of social and extracurricular activities at State University. Tyler didn't pledge a fraternity, study abroad, take a leadership role in any of the professional organizations for business students, or actively participate in other extracurricular activities.

Did you know?

More than 73% of employers say they have screened college applicants by GPA.[3]

By not participating, Tyler has missed out on a lot of fun and memorable experiences, but that's not all. He also didn't get a chance to make friends as well as future business and social contacts through those types of activities. Furthermore, he lacks an extracurricular record at State University that could help him stand out to potential employers and graduate schools. When Tyler graduates, he likely won't be well positioned for the job market or graduate school.

Contrast Tyler's college experience with Mason's. This is Mason's final semester. He's about to graduate a semester early, thanks to the college credit he earned before starting at State University. Finishing college early will save Mason a lot of money and allow him to further minimize his student loan debt. He will graduate with academic honors and a high GPA because he used a careful strategy to maximize the grades he earned at State University. Mason has two job offers: one from a hot startup whose founder is an alumnus of his fraternity, and another from the global company where he interned last summer. If he decides to go to graduate school, he'll have the strong undergraduate record that the top schools require.

For Mason, college hasn't been just about studying. He's worked hard, but he's also played hard. Getting off to a good start his freshman year has made a huge difference in his college experience. Unlike Tyler, he hasn't had to work overtime to raise his GPA after a rocky start. That has allowed him to spend more time on other important aspects of college life that fall outside the classroom.

He's had a great social life, and he's been very involved in extracurricular activities. Mason pledged a fraternity. He plays on a rugby club team. He holds a leadership role in a student organization for business majors. He studied abroad. He did multiple internships. These experiences have been more than just fun and good for his résumé. In addition to providing a valuable education that goes beyond academics, they have helped Mason build a network of potentially useful business and social connections.

Did you know?

More than ½ of all college graduates under the age of 25 are either jobless or underemployed.[4]

Let's be clear. Tyler and Mason both studied—a lot. But while Tyler worked harder than he ever did in high school, only to achieve disappointing results, Mason excelled by working smarter. By taking a strategic approach to college rather than relying on willpower and sweat alone, Mason has been academically successful, enjoyed a variety of experiences, and had a lot of fun. And best of all, after he graduates, he'll be well positioned to succeed. For Mason, the future only gets brighter.

Why This Book?

If you're like the vast majority of students, you want to be more like Mason than Tyler. You want more than just a quality education that prepares you for life after college. You want great grades and a high GPA. You want to tackle the course requirements for your degree efficiently so that you can graduate on time. Along the way, you want to have fun, make friends and contacts, and create awesome memories. And no matter what else happens, you want to complete college cost-effectively, without depleting your parents' life savings or burdening yourself with a mountain of student loan debt.

Longer term, you want to use college as a stepping-stone to open doors. Doors to job opportunities with top-rated employers that get your career off on a great trajectory. Doors to outstanding graduate schools in the field where you will eventually pursue a career. Doors that position you for a bright future and the kind of life you want to lead.

As we saw in the story of Tyler and Mason, though, getting good grades and graduating from college on time isn't easy, even for students who aced high school. Unfortunately, lots of public university students—including many who were strong high school students and academically prepared for college—don't graduate with a college GPA anywhere close to what they achieved in high school. Furthermore, many of those same students don't graduate from college on time.

Did you know?

Only 58% of students with an A to A+ average in high school graduate from college in 4 years.[5]

Universities are very different from high schools. You need to do more than just study and make the effort to get good grades and graduate on time. To ace the public university, you need a strategy.

Creating a winning college strategy on your own isn't easy. Even the best high schools rarely prepare students for the very different rules of college academics. High schools focus on providing students like you with the book smarts you need to enter college, not on teaching you a strategic approach that can help you maximize your college GPA and ensure that you'll graduate on time.

You can't count on public universities to teach you these skills, either, for a variety of reasons. When it comes to this kind of information, you're usually entirely on your own and forced to learn the hard way through trial and error.

The GPAMaxx Perspective

At GPAMaxx®, we think too many students are too much like Tyler and not enough like Mason. We strongly believe that too many students at public universities fail to get the highest grades they are capable of and fail to graduate on time. For many of these students, this isn't because they lack the raw intelligence, academic preparation, or determination to succeed, but rather because they make three fundamental errors:

- **Inability to approach college strategically.** Many students don't understand how the rules of college differ from those for high school. Consequently, they don't develop a strategic approach to college that allows them to thrive academically and puts them on track to graduate on time.

- **Lack of planning.** Many students don't develop and then regularly update a university game plan that details how they will complete the course requirements they need to get a degree, causing them to make serious errors that hurt their grades and delay their graduation.

- **Failure to select courses conducive to getting the high grades they are capable of achieving.** Many students don't know how to select university courses that allow them to shine academically and maximize their GPA.

These errors prevent many college students from living up to their potential. They don't ever become high-achieving college students, and they don't graduate on time. As a result, not only is college more expensive, less fulfilling, and—often—a lot less fun for these students, but they can face a narrowed range of career and graduate school opportunities after they graduate.

The GPAMaxx Solution

At GPAMaxx, we have a different way of approaching undergraduate education. In this book, we teach you how to approach your studies strategically, so that you can position yourself to get the best possible grades and graduate on time, or even early. Our goal: to help you become a student more like Mason and less like Tyler.

First, we provide you with the background information you'll need to successfully navigate the university you plan to attend. Then we teach you how to apply an approach we've developed, the GPAMaxx Strategy™, that can help you maximize your college GPA and graduate on time—or early.

The GPAMaxx Strategy lets you tackle college in a way that allows you to maximize your academic strengths and minimize your academic weaknesses. Its step-by-step approaches help you complete your degree requirements efficiently and, often, more cost-effectively.

We can't guarantee that by applying what you'll learn here and using the GPAMaxx Strategy, you will always get the high grades you want and will graduate on time. That's up to you. But combined with hard work on your part, a more strategic approach to college can help you better position yourself for success in college and a bright future afterward.

Your college years are your time to shine. So keep reading and begin your journey to college success.

What's in This Book?

To teach you our approach, we have organized this book into
seven parts:

Part I: Why You Need Your Own College Strategy introduces
you to the GPAMaxx Strategy and discusses why you need to
approach college strategically and take the lead role in shaping
your university career.

Part II: Demystifying the Grade Game focuses on multiple
aspects of grading at public universities and their implications
for you.

Part III: Getting to Know Your University Road Map teaches
you the basics of your degree plan, the road map to your
university degree.

Part IV: Two Key Strategies for Acing the Public University
introduces two strategic alternatives to taking courses at your
university, credit by examination and transfer courses, and it
shows you how you can use them to your benefit in a number
of ways.

Part V: Getting to Know Yourself shows you the importance
of recognizing your strengths, weaknesses, and preferences
as a student and how to factor in those considerations as you
develop your university game plan and choose your courses.

Part VI: Learning to Professor Shop teaches you to
determine how professors will likely grade the students in
your potential courses, an essential consideration for finding
well-suited courses.

Part VII: Applying the GPAMaxx Strategy shows you in step-
by-step fashion how to apply each part of the GPAMaxx Strategy.
You learn how to apply the GPAMaxx Game Plan Module™, our
framework to help you create your own university game plan,
and how you can use the GPAMaxx Course Selection Module™
to find GPA-friendly courses that are a good fit for you and
count toward your degree.

Who Is This Book For?

As the title indicates, this book is for anyone who attends or may eventually attend—even several years in the future—a public university. It provides valuable insights and guidance to high school students and others who intend to study at a public university, and to current public university students. Although these audiences are often close in age, they can be worlds apart in many other respects. Let's look at how this book can help each group.

- **Current high school students who may attend a public university.** At GPAMaxx, we don't believe that the best time to learn about the rules of college academics is at first-semester orientation. That's like getting behind the wheel for a long road trip before you've even taken driver's ed. The best time to learn about how college works, and to start developing your own college game plan, is long before you start. For high school seniors, juniors, and even ambitious sophomores, reading this book and acting on what you learn can help you set the stage for your future success at a public university.

  After reading this book, you'll more clearly understand how college academics work and what you need to do to be a strong student and get your degree. This will make your transition to college easier.

  We'll also show you how to develop a game plan now—in high school—to succeed at college. You can follow our step-by-step approach to learn on your own about the college course requirements you'll eventually need to fulfill at the university you hope to attend. This will help you select the high school courses that will best prepare you for your college classes. Better still, by developing a college game plan using the step-by-step process you'll learn here, you can maximize the amount of college-level credit that you can earn while still in high school. In some cases, that credit can provide a big head start on completing your college degree, saving you a lot of time and money in the process. (Much more on this later.)

And finally, when the time comes to select courses for your first semester of college, you can use another step-by-step process you'll learn here to help you find the courses that count toward your degree, seem a good fit, and offer you a greater chance to earn the high grades you want. By carefully selecting your courses, you'll minimize the risk of taking courses during your first semester that don't count toward your degree or that are a poor fit. All of this can help you get off to a strong start at college and put you on track to graduate on time.

- **Incoming and current public university students.** Whether you're about to start college or already have a few semesters under your belt, this book can help you. Some sections offer advice to students who have yet to begin college, but most of the book can be of enormous help if you've already started. Wherever you are in your college career, it's important for you to understand exactly how college academics work, to develop your own custom-tailored college game plan that maps out your route toward graduating on time, and to learn to select courses that both count toward your degree and improve your chances to earn the high grades you want. This book can help you with all of these.

No matter which of these audiences you belong to, this book can help you, now and in the future. We assume that you are motivated, want to be a great college student, want to graduate on time, and want to position yourself for a bright future after college. But don't think for a second that we've written this book for only one kind of student. It's designed for students of varying academic abilities. Maybe you have taken or currently take some Advanced Placement, International Baccalaureate, or other advanced-level college-prep courses in high school. Or perhaps you are (or were) in regular-level high school courses. Regardless of what type of student you've been until now, this book can help you build the foundation for success in college.

A Word to Parents

Although we wrote this book to help prospective and current public university students, we recognize that many parents are reading it, too. We know you want your child to succeed at college. But many smart, college-ready students make big strategic errors—both in their academic planning for college and once they actually start—that can limit their opportunities, have serious negative financial consequences, and keep them from realizing their full potential. This book can help make sure that doesn't happen.

You can also play a part. Get involved in your child's college planning now, and stay involved. Put yourself in an informed position to more effectively help your child, both before and during college. Start by reading this book and making sure your son or daughter reads it. Learn the strategic approaches we teach, and work with your child to help maximize his or her potential.

Sound like a lot? It can be. But college can set the stage for life. And for your child to excel at college and position himself or herself for a bright future afterward, your involvement could be vital. Even a little involvement can go a long way. So whatever you do, get involved.

How to Use This Book

To get the most out of this book, we suggest reading it from beginning to end at least once. After that, you can refer to particular sections when the need arises. Trying to understand the different ways to calculate your GPA and the implications for you? Take a look at "GPA Explained" in Chapter 3. Seeking to better understand potential strategic alternatives to taking a course at your own university? Turn to Part IV. And when you design your own university game plan and pick your college courses, you can follow the step-by-step approaches in Part VII. Think of this book not only as a handbook to prepare you for college, but as a handy reference guide for your entire college journey.

Why You Need Your Own College Strategy

Too many students don't realize the importance of developing a strategic approach to college and taking the lead role in their college planning. This causes them to make mistakes—often preventable ones—that not only hurt their grades and prevent them from graduating on time, but limit the opportunities open to them when they graduate.

Part I provides an overview of the GPAMaxx Strategy and explains how it can help you develop a university game plan and pick the courses that best position you to get good grades. You also learn why you shouldn't rely on your university and its academic advisors for your academic planning decisions. Instead, we'll show you why you need to take the lead role so that you can make decisions that are in your own best interest.

By the end of Part I, you'll be well positioned to start learning how to approach college from a more strategic angle.

The GPAMaxx Strategy: A First Look

This Chapter Covers

- Why you need a college strategy
- Introduction to the GPAMaxx Strategy
- Introduction to the GPAMaxx Cardinal Rules

Imagine you're attending freshman orientation at your university. You're in a room with nine other students and an orientation counselor, who points out some sobering statistics about your school. She tells you that on average, only three-quarters of you will return for sophomore year. She goes on to say that only 4 of the 10 of you will likely graduate within four years, only 6 within five years, and only 7 within six years.

You might find those grim numbers hard to believe, but the actual averages for public university students generally are even lower. More than 27 percent of public university freshmen don't return to their universities for their sophomore year, according to one study. At two-year public institutions like community colleges, an even smaller percentage—slightly more than half of first-year students— returns for a second year.[6]

And when public university students do graduate, only 31.3 percent of public university students graduate in four years, 50.6 percent within five years, and 56 percent within six years, according to one report.[7]

In all likelihood, though, those odds probably don't faze you a bit. Why? You're positive you'll be one of the students who return for sophomore year. You're sure that you'll be one of the four students in the room who graduate on time in four years. Washing out of college or not graduating on time happens to other students, not to you.

If you are like many students who excelled in high school, you may also assume that you'll repeat your strong high school performance in college. After all, as your parents and everyone at your high school has told you time and again, you're well prepared for college-level work. You took all those college prep classes, and you're willing to put in the hard work required to be successful at college. So why wouldn't you continue to get the high grades you've come to expect?

Did you know?

Less than ⅓ of all public university students graduate in 4 years, and barely ½ graduate in 5.

Unfortunately, there's a lot more to getting high grades at college and graduating on time than just hitting the books and putting in the hours at the library. College is very different from high school, with new and very different rules. Too many—if not most—high school students arrive for their first semester of college mired in the high school mindset. They still believe in the old high school notion that effort equals results—that if they study hard enough and do exactly what they're told, they'll get good grades and graduate from college on time.

For most of you, though, the high school approach won't get you the grades you have come to expect, nor will it ensure that you graduate from college on time. If you attend one of your state's more selective public universities, it's likely everyone else there also got close to straight As in high school. College is an entirely different ballgame. To thrive, you must not only take your game to another level. You must change how you play it.

We wrote this book to help you better understand the rules of the new college game and to teach you a strategy to play by: the GPAMaxx Strategy™. We designed the GPAMaxx Strategy to help you achieve two main objectives:

- **Maximize your college GPA**

- **Graduate from college on time—or early**

Using the GPAMaxx Strategy can fundamentally change the way you approach college. You adopt a more strategic mindset. You find ways to complete your degree requirements efficiently and, often, more cost-effectively. You learn how to select well-fitting courses. By approaching college in a strategic manner, you better position yourself to maximize your grades, graduate on time, have a more positive experience both in and outside the classroom, and use college as a springboard to a successful future.

We organized this book to teach this strategic approach to college. Parts I through VI will educate you about some of the most important aspects of public university academics. We'll show you how to approach them strategically, with an eye to maximizing your grades and completing your degree requirements efficiently. Armed with this information, you'll have the know-how that you need to apply the GPAMaxx Strategy successfully. Then, in Part VII, you learn how to apply the GPAMaxx Strategy on your own. We'll provide you with step-by-step modules that you can use to develop a college game plan and choose well-suited courses.

For now, let's take a quick walk through what the GPAMaxx Strategy is and how it works.

The GPAMaxx Strategy: A Brief Overview

The GPAMaxx Strategy consists of two parts: the GPAMaxx Game Plan Module™ and the GPAMaxx Course Selection Module™. We cover each in detail in Part VII. The following is a brief introduction to each of these modules and an explanation of how they can help you.

The GPAMaxx Game Plan Module

The first part of the GPAMaxx Strategy is the **GPAMaxx Game Plan Module**. This is a step-by-step guide to creating your own university game plan that maps out how you can complete your degree requirements. By working your way through a series of nine steps, you develop your own strategy for fulfilling your degree requirements in a manner that's efficient and, often, more cost-effective and GPA-friendly. As you progress through your college career, you will update your game plan regularly.

How It Can Help You

Many college students don't pay nearly enough attention to how they will fulfill the course requirements they need to get their degree. Navigating the maze of requirements can be really tricky, especially if you don't have a game plan. As a result, lots of college students make planning errors that hurt their grades and ultimately prevent them from graduating on time.

The GPAMaxx Game Plan Module minimizes these and other risks. This nine-step approach will help you understand what you have to do to complete the requirements of your degree, as well as the options you have to fulfill them. It can also prevent you from making mistakes that can hurt your grades and keep you from graduating on time.

The GPAMaxx Game Plan Module: A Sneak Preview

You'll learn how to develop your own university game plan in Chapter 16. For now, though, here's a brief look at the nine steps you work through to develop your custom-tailored university game plan.

Step 1: Find out your university's requirements to graduate with academic honors.

Step 2: Get and review a copy of your degree plan (the document that sets forth all the course requirements you must complete to graduate from your university).

Step 3: Familiarize yourself with the rules and policies relating to the completion of your degree.

Step 4: Evaluate where you currently stand (in completing your degree requirements).

Step 5: Evaluate what you already know (in the courses required for your degree).

Step 6: Discover strategic alternatives to taking courses at your university.

Step 7: Create a credit by examination action plan.

Step 8: Create a transfer course action plan.

Step 9: Create and update your own ongoing university master game plan.

Don't know exactly what we're referring to in each step above? Not to worry. After you read this book, you will.

The GPAMaxx Course Selection Module

The second part of the GPAMaxx Strategy is the **GPAMaxx Course Selection Module**, a step-by-step approach we've developed to help you select your courses each semester. Following this module will help you find well-fitting courses and fulfill your degree requirements efficiently.

How It Can Help You

Most college students don't get the high grades that could better position them for a successful future after graduation. For many, that's not because they are poorly prepared for college-level work, or are lazy, or treat college as a never-ending party. In fact, many spend huge amounts of time studying and preparing for their classes, but they still don't get the results they want. A big reason: these students don't know how to find the courses that position them to shine academically.

That shouldn't be too surprising. After all, only rarely does anyone teach students a strategic approach to selecting the university courses that are a good fit for them. As a result, many students never learn how to do this. Semester after semester, year after year, they overlook better options for fulfilling their degree requirements and suffer through courses that are a bad fit for them—and their GPAs. These poorly thought-out course selections hurt their grades and keep students from maximizing their potential at college, both academically and otherwise.

The GPAMaxx Course Selection Module helps you minimize the risk of becoming one of these students. Using it lets you more fully comprehend all the choices you have to complete your degree requirements. This helps you select well-fitting courses and make better, more informed decisions about how to fulfill those requirements.

The GPAMaxx Cardinal Rules

As you go through this book, you will learn how to apply three core principles that will help you approach your studies strategically and maximize your grades. These three principles, called the GPAMaxx Cardinal Rules™, are:

- GPAMaxx Cardinal Rule #1:
  Know Your University Road Map—Your Degree Plan

- GPAMaxx Cardinal Rule #2:
  Know Yourself as a Student

- GPAMaxx Cardinal Rule #3:
  Know How to Professor Shop

Understanding how to apply each of these principles will also give you much of the background you need to apply the GPAMaxx Strategy successfully on your own. We explore them in detail later in this book.

Not Graduating on Time: Your Real Dollar Cost

Earlier in this chapter, we mentioned that less than a third of students at public universities graduate on time within four years, and just slightly over half finish within five. What we didn't mention is how much money taking even a single extra year to graduate can cost you.

First, there are an extra year's worth of tuition and fees. For the 2014–15 academic year, tuition and fees for in-state students at public universities averaged $9,139. That doesn't include room and board, books, supplies, transportation, and various other expenses. Those outlays can bring the average cost of an extra year to more than $23,400.[8]

(continued on following page)

That's a big expenditure for you and/or your parents to shoulder, and, for many of you, a lot more student loan debt. But it's not the full cost of failing to graduate on time. You also have to consider the wages that you miss out on by postponing your entrance into the workforce. This is where the bottom line really starts to balloon.

Let's look at an example to give you an idea of the real cost of an extra year of college:

Say you're a student from Virginia who returns to the University of Virginia for a fifth year instead of graduating on time. For the 2014–15 academic year, tuition and fees for returning in-state students there averaged $13,216 to $18,084 (depending on their major), while estimated costs for room and board, textbooks and supplies, and personal expenses averaged $13,748.[9] Those amounts total $26,964 to $31,832. Meanwhile, the average starting annual salary for University of Virginia graduates is around $51,000.[10]

If you were working instead of spending an extra year on campus, earning the average annual starting salary, your take-home pay—even after taxes—would be over $35,000. And you wouldn't be spending money on tuition, textbooks, or any of the other expenditures you incur as a college student. Taken together, your extra year of college could easily cost you $50,000, if not more. That's enough for a down payment on a house, a lengthy trip around the world, or a brand-new BMW.

Seeing the potential financial impact of that fifth year might be all the motivation you need to graduate on time. If it isn't, find out for yourself how much money not graduating on time from your university could potentially cost you. Doing this may persuade you to develop your own university game plan to graduate within four years, with your finances intact.

Academic Advising: Why You Need to Look Out for Yourself

This Chapter Covers

- The significant limitations of academic advisors at public universities
- Why you need to be your own best academic advisor

Imagine you're making a decision that could have big consequences for your future and possibly even alter the course of your life. You'd spend at least a little time learning what you need to know so you could make an informed decision, wouldn't you? Given that your future is at stake, you'd want to be the one who makes the decision, not leave it to someone who might barely know you and has absolutely no idea about your unique strengths, weaknesses, and preferences.

And yet every semester, large numbers of college students fail to consider those big consequences when they register for their courses. Even though their college grades can play a huge role in shaping their futures, many students don't sufficiently investigate on their own the courses they register for. As a result, they select courses that are poorly suited to them for one reason or another. Not surprisingly, they often earn lousy grades in those courses. Instead of doing research in advance to find courses that are a good fit, too many students simply follow the advice of the academic advisor their university assigns to them, without questioning the merits of the advice even for a minute.

Although academic advising differs from campus to campus, an advisor's job nearly always includes advising students on their selection of courses and related issues. Your advisor may be a faculty member in your proposed major, or perhaps a full-time academic advisor at an on-campus advising center.

Your advisor can be a terrific asset for you when you use his or her advice correctly. But unfortunately, far too many students overly depend on their advisors' suggestions instead of developing their own university game plans. They don't independently research their course requirements and the different ways they can fulfill them. Instead, these students simply assume that their academic advisor will lead them by the hand. Many even expect their advisors to choose their classes and all but plan their route to graduation.

Did you know?

On average, each full-time public university academic advisor is responsible for 285 students.[11]

Although academic advisors often provide valuable guidance and can be a great resource, over-relying on them can be detrimental to your GPA and your university career. You, not your academic advisor, need to take the lead role in your college planning. You, not your advisor, must develop a university game plan and find the courses that best fit you. It is your responsibility to thoroughly understand the requirements you must complete to graduate and to learn about the various ways you may fulfill them. Unless you educate yourself about your options, you may end up following poor advice from your academic advisor—with no one to blame but yourself.

Why You Need to Be Your Own Best Academic Advisor

We wouldn't be surprised if you disagreed with us about the importance of being your own academic advisor. You're probably thinking, "Academic advisors have a far greater familiarity than I do with the requirements to complete my degree, as well as the inner workings of the university. How can I possibly know better what's best for me when it comes to my studies?" Regardless of whether this is true, you need to take the lead and become your own best academic advisor. Here are some of the reasons:

Enormous Caseloads

At many universities, each academic advisor works with hundreds of students. As a result, advisors don't often have time to become familiar with each student's individual profile in any depth. In fact, at many universities, you're likely to meet with your advisor only once or twice a semester, if that often. You might see your advisor for 10 minutes the week before you register for your courses each semester. Do you think he spends any time thinking about the ones you should take before you walk into his office? Probably not.

You Know You Best

Academic advisors are rarely in a position to offer advice that's custom tailored to fit you and your unique situation. Given how overloaded academic advisors are at most public universities, to expect otherwise is unrealistic. Even if you're fortunate enough to develop a good working relationship with your academic advisor, you still shouldn't expect her to know your strengths and weaknesses as well as you do yourself. It's unlikely that she will be capable of providing you with highly personalized advice.

Do consider what your advisor has to say, but never let her advice replace your own research, instincts, and judgment regarding your academic game plan and which courses are most suitable for you and your GPA. You need to understand yourself as a student and your degree requirements well enough to have a good sense of what's best for you.

No One Knows Everything

Even if your advisor is a professor in your major, he may still have only a very basic knowledge of all the courses offered each semester. A communications major focusing on speech pathology may be assigned to an advisor who teaches mass media—or the other way around. And if your advisor is part of the campus advisory service, you really can't expect him to know much more about each course than its name and whatever brief description appears on the university's website.

At most public universities, you may have more options to fulfill your degree requirements than you think. For example, you can bypass some courses completely by testing out of them (a process called credit by examination, or CBE). Or you can take courses at other colleges if your university will count them toward your degree. Unfortunately, your advisor may not be on top of the multiple ways you can fulfill degree requirements outside of your university's own classrooms. He's naturally going to be far more familiar with the standard course offerings at your university than with alternate options.

For all of the above reasons, you need to take the lead on matters like these. After all, you're the person with the vested interest in finding out all the details about the things that affect your college career—not your advisor. You have to live with the consequences; he doesn't.

Maximizing Your GPA Is Not the Priority

Don't look to your academic advisor for help designing a university game plan or picking courses in ways that help you maximize your GPA. That simply isn't part of her job description.

Think about it: is it reasonable to expect her to show you how to navigate the requirements of your degree so that you can take the GPA-friendliest courses for you? Or to tell you not to take Introduction to Sociology with Professor Jones because he's a harsh grader, and instead take it with Professor Chen because she typically gives As to over half of her students?

Of course not. It's your responsibility to find out that kind of information on your own.

Conflicts of Interest

Too many students assume that their advisors always have the best interests of students at heart. They forget that the university employs academic advisors and expects them to look out for the university's interests first and foremost. And in some instances, the real potential exists for a conflict of interest in the advice they may give.

For example, your academic advisor might steer you toward courses offered at your university even when you might be better off taking the equivalent course at a different college during your summer break. Or he might persuade you to enroll in your university's own study abroad program, even though an unaffiliated program might be cheaper, a better fit, or both.

There are many reasons to try to keep you on campus and maintain the continuous flow of your tuition dollars. From an administrative viewpoint, helping students pursue alternative course options usually equals more paperwork and bureaucratic headaches for your advisor and the university. Anything that takes extra time and effort equals increased costs to the university.

More significantly, taking courses at other colleges usually causes your university to lose out on the tuition you would have paid for those courses. In particular, the department that houses your major may be adversely affected, because its funding depends at least in part on enrollment in courses offered on campus. Especially in majors with few students, you may find that a very small number of students enroll in those courses. If a minimum number of students don't sign up for a particular course, it can be cancelled altogether. Fewer students can equal less funding for affected departments, and less funding can ultimately result in fewer teaching positions.

Given all that's at stake, it's easy to see how these financial considerations can influence the advice your academic advisor gives you. The instinct for self-preservation might prompt your advisor to recommend courses on campus, or to dissuade you from taking advantage of more potentially suitable options. At the very least, your advisor might not remind you to explore all the other options you have to fulfill degree requirements. But unless you have adequately informed yourself about your full range of options, you won't be in a good position to assess the advice and make the best decisions for you.

Working with Your Academic Advisor

To be clear, we aren't telling you to blow off your advisor, or to disregard everything he has to say. Academic advisors are valuable resources, so you should certainly consult with them on a regular basis. But you should carefully evaluate their advice, armed with an understanding of the course requirements you need to fulfill in order to graduate as well as a sense of your academic strengths, weaknesses, and preferences. Ideally, you want to position yourself to critically evaluate your advisor's advice alongside the information you collect yourself, and then make the decisions that are in your best interest. After all, you are a unique person with your own strengths, weaknesses, and goals. The better informed you are and the clearer the university game plan you develop, the more you can leverage your advisor's expertise and knowledge to help you.

PART II

Demystifying the Grade Game

The different aspects of university grading are a mystery to many incoming college students. All too often, new college students don't understand exactly how college-level grading works. They don't know how instructors decide the types of grades students earn, or how a GPA gets calculated. Even if they recognize why grades and a high GPA are so important to their future, they may not know exactly what kind of GPA they will need to graduate with honors and position themselves for the bright future they want.

The chapters in Part II shed light on each of those issues in detail. Though we approach things as if you have yet to start college, Part II is still useful to current university students. Wherever you are in the process, it's important for you to understand university-level grading and what it means for you.

After you read Part II, you'll understand grades and grading at universities and the implications for you. This will better position you to make the choices that allow you to maximize your academic potential.

3

Grades and GPAs:
The Basics

This Chapter Covers

- Letter and non-letter grading
- Academic calendars explained
- How credit hours work
- Two important types of GPA and how they're calculated
- Understanding the impact of low grades on your GPA

As in high school, your grades in college will likely be the primary yardstick used to measure and judge your overall performance as a student. For each course you take, your final grade usually consists of a letter grade that's translated into a number, known as a **grade point**. Your **grade point average**, or **GPA**, is the numerical measure of your overall academic performance; it consists of the calculated average of the grade points that you earn.

Letter Grading

Generally speaking, letter grades at public universities correspond to the grade points on the scale below:

Letter Grade	Numerical Grade (Quality) Points
A	4.0
A−	3.67
B+	3.33
B	3.0
B−	2.67
C+	2.33
C	2.0
C−	1.67
D+	1.33
D	1.0
D−	0.67
F	0

Your university may set its grade cutoffs a little differently—its A− may be 3.75 and its B+ 3.50. Some universities don't have plus or minus grades, so an A is a 4.0, a B is a 3.0, and so on, with nothing in between.

Some universities also award a grade of A+, which sometimes gets assigned the grade point of 4.33. At other universities, an A+ only counts as 4.0. Under the typical U.S. university grading scale, an A or an A+ is the highest passing grade, and a D or a D− is the lowest passing grade. No grade points are awarded for any course in which you get a grade of F, which is always a failing grade.

Pass/Fail Grading

In some courses at your university, you may receive a grade that doesn't get averaged into your GPA at all, as long as you pass the course or receive a grade above a certain level (a C, for example). Universities offer a variety of courses graded on this basis, which may be called by a number of names, including Pass/Fail, Credit/No Credit, Satisfactory/Unsatisfactory, and Pass/No Pass. Some courses are only graded this way; in others you can elect to be graded pass/fail rather than receive a letter grade. The exact rules for this type of grading designation can vary from university to university.

University Academic Calendars: The Semester vs. the Quarter System

Academic calendars usually operate on one of two systems: the semester and the quarter. Universities with **semesters** typically divide the academic year into two primary terms, fall and spring, each around 15 weeks long. Universities on the **quarter** system typically divide the academic year into fall, winter, and spring quarters, each about 10 weeks long. In both semesters and quarters, the total number of instructional weeks in an academic year is around 30.

Most universities use the semester system, so all references and examples in this book assume a semester, not a quarter.

Credit Hours

Most university degree programs require students to earn course credits equivalent to eight full semesters, or four academic years of full-time study. These units of study are broken down into a time measurement known as a **credit hour**. Universities typically require students to complete a certain number of credit hours, sometimes referred to as units, in order to graduate.

Credit hours are normally based on the number of hours of actual instruction per week, although this isn't always the case (for example, courses with a laboratory component or a discussion section may involve more hours of instruction than credit). Typically, a course that meets for around three hours each week is worth three credit hours.

The minimum number of credit hours you need to graduate depends on which university you attend as well as your specific major, but it rarely falls below 120 credit hours. Most universities recommend that students take a course load each semester that

Too Much of a Good Thing: The Excess Credit Hour Problem

While poor planning causes many students to lack the required number of credit hours they need to graduate on time, it causes a different problem for other students: they complete far too many credit hours before they graduate. Nationwide, students rack up an average of 136.5 credit hours toward degrees that require only 120 credit hours to complete.[12] A common culprit: courses that aren't required for their degrees. As a result of taking even a few such courses, much like the students who take too few courses each semester, many of these students also don't graduate on time.

Don't do this. Develop a college game plan that ensures you complete only coursework that counts toward your degree, and not a credit hour more.

enables them to graduate in the equivalent of eight semesters over four years. If your degree requires 120 credit hours, for example, that breaks down to 15 credit hours for each of eight semesters.

However, many universities only require their students to carry a minimum of 12 credit hours in a semester to be considered a full-time student. You don't have to be a math major to realize that it may take you longer than eight semesters to graduate if you carry only 12 credit hours per semester. Every semester, some students take only the minimum instead of the recommended number of credit hours. As a result, they don't graduate on time in four years. If you choose to take less than your school's recommended full-time course load during any semester, always make sure you remain on track to graduate on time.

How Credit Hours Tie into Grades

For each credit hour you complete, you receive a set number of grade points based on the grade you receive in each course.

That means if you take Introduction to Psychology, a three-credit-hour course, you receive three times the grade points you earn for it. If you earn an A, which corresponds to 4.0 grade points, you receive a total of 12.0 grade points. Table 3–1 shows how the number of grade points for each course grade is calculated using this example.

Table 3-1

Course at State University	Credit Hours	Letter Grade	Grade Points for Letter Grade	Total Number of Grade Points for Course
Introduction to Psychology	3	A	4.0	12.0

Credit hours	×	Grade points awarded for letter grade	=	Total number of grade points for course
3.0		4.0		12.0

GPA Explained

At its most basic level, your GPA is simply the average number of grade points for all your courses. To calculate this average, divide the total of your grade points by the total number of credit hours you complete.

Table 3–2 shows the calculation of one student's GPA in a single semester.

Table 3-2

Course at State University	Credit Hours	Letter Grade	Grade Points for Letter Grade	Total Number of Grade Points for Course
Principles of Macroeconomics	3	A	4.0	12.0
Introduction to Chemistry	4	C	2.0	8.0
First-Semester Japanese	5	A–	3.7	18.5
U.S. History to 1877	3	B+	3.3	9.9

Total credit hours earned toward graduation 15

Total grade points earned. 48.4

Total grade points earned	÷	Total credit hours earned toward graduation	=	GPA
48.4		15		3.227

Calculating a GPA can seem simple, but it involves a lot more than just doing math. You need to understand two especially important types of GPA, how they get calculated, and what they mean for you.

Cumulative GPA vs. Institutional GPA

Let's have a closer look at two important types of GPA that every student has: a cumulative and an institutional GPA.

Cumulative GPA

First, let's talk about a metric called the **cumulative GPA**. There are different terms for this type of GPA, but conceptually they're all the same thing.

Your cumulative GPA is the average of all the grade points and credit hours from every course you take at any college, whether you take them at your university or some other college. If you apply to graduate school, the cumulative GPA is the one that the admissions office will likely consider in determining whether to admit you.

Institutional GPA

Another important type of GPA is sometimes called the **institutional GPA**. Again, the term used to describe it may differ depending on the university, but we use institutional GPA throughout this book.

Your institutional GPA is your GPA as calculated by your university. A majority of public universities generally include only the grades from their own courses in this calculation. Grades from courses taken at other colleges, meanwhile, get excluded entirely from the institutional GPA.

Many schools in this majority do make some exceptions when they calculate the institutional GPA, though. Some universities, for example, include grades from courses students take at partner universities in study abroad programs. Others include grades that students earn in courses at other universities in the same university system. For example, if a student attends the University of California, Los Angeles, the grades she earns in courses taken at any other campus in the University of California system still count toward her institutional GPA. There can be other exceptions as well.

By contrast, a sizeable minority of public universities take yet another approach. These schools include the grades from courses taken at any college in the institutional GPA calculation, which leaves no distinction between the institutional and cumulative GPAs.

Sound confusing? It can be, especially because university approaches vary so widely. This makes it crucial for you to find out exactly how your university calculates your institutional GPA.

Cumulative vs. Institutional GPA: Why the Distinction Matters

As we mentioned above, most graduate schools' admissions offices will look at your cumulative GPA when deciding whether to admit you. So if you apply to graduate school, they'll consider all your grades, regardless of where you earned them. For multiple reasons, however, your institutional GPA is the GPA you especially want to focus on maximizing.

Your institutional GPA is the one your university calculates, so it's the one that always appears on your transcript. As a result, it's the GPA that potential employers and anyone else will likely see if they review your transcript. Your institutional GPA is also likely the one your university uses to determine your eligibility for things like GPA-dependent scholarships and admission to certain university honors programs.

Finally, when your university determines whether you graduate with honors based on your GPA, more often than not, it will consider only your institutional GPA, not your cumulative GPA. For these reasons, you'll want to make an extra effort to maximize your institutional GPA.

When you understand how your university calculates your institutional GPA, you can fulfill your course requirements in ways that allow you to maximize your institutional GPA. Suppose, for example, that you study at a university that includes only its own course grades in calculating your institutional GPA. If you expect a particular course to be difficult for you, you can take it at a different college. The credit hours for the course at the other college will count toward your degree, but the grade you earn in it won't have any impact on your institutional GPA.

This can be a huge benefit to you. It means the C you earn in the chemistry class that you take as a visiting student at a community college won't hurt your institutional GPA. You get credit hours toward your degree and satisfy a course requirement, but that low grade doesn't drag down your institutional GPA. Whenever you suspect you might have a hard time earning a good grade in a particular course, it can make a lot of sense to take the equivalent course at a different college.

Nothing Lasts Forever, but Bad Grades Come Awfully Close

Calculating your GPA is fairly easy, but that simplicity masks some hard truths.

You may not fully grasp, for example, the extent to which a single low grade can drastically lower what would otherwise be a high GPA. (For discussion purposes, we consider a "low" grade anything below a B). If you're striving to graduate with a high institutional GPA and the academic honors that can come with it, the low number of grade points awarded for any grade below a B can make it enormously difficult to recover. On the next page, you'll see just how severely even a single low course grade negatively impacts a very high GPA.

Learning by Example

Here's a story that shows you just how devastating a single poor course grade can be on even a strong student's GPA.

In his first semester at State University, Noah earned the following grades and GPA:

Course at State University	Credit Hours	Letter Grade	Grade Points for Letter Grade	Total Number of Grade Points for Course
Introduction to Cultural Anthropology	3	A	4.0	12.0
Composition I	3	A	4.0	12.0
Introduction to Ethics	3	A	4.0	12.0
U.S. History to 1877	3	A	4.0	12.0
Physical Science I	3	D	1.0	3.0

Total credit hours earned toward graduation 15

Total grade points earned. 51.0

Total grade points earned	÷	Total credit hours earned toward graduation	=	GPA
51.0		4.0		3.4

The result: Noah earned a GPA of 3.4 for his first semester. Unfortunately, a single D brought Noah's GPA down from a perfect 4.0 to a 3.4. That's the same GPA he would have had if he had earned three Bs and only two As.

At many public universities, that average won't put Noah in contention to graduate with GPA-based honors unless he raises his GPA in future semesters. And that will be no small task. Let's say he wants to raise his GPA to 3.7 by the end of his second semester and will again take 15 credit hours worth of courses. Here's how we determine the GPA that Noah would need in his second semester to accomplish this:

Desired GPA by end of Noah's 2nd semester = 3.7

STEP 1	Desired GPA	×	Total number of credit hours for 1st and 2nd semesters	=	Total number of grade points
	3.7		30		111

STEP 2	Total number of grade points	−	Grade points from 1st semester	=	Grade points needed for 2nd semester
	111		51		60

STEP 3	Grade points needed for 2nd semester	÷	Number of credit hours for 2nd semester	=	Required 2nd semester GPA
	60		15		4

GPA required to earn in 2nd semester to achieve overall 3.7 GPA = 4.0

As the above calculations illustrate, Noah will need a 4.0 (an A) in each of his second-semester courses just to raise his overall GPA to a 3.7. That one poor grade—a D in Physical Science I—requires him to make As in 27 credit hours, or nine courses of three credit hours each, just to have a 3.7 GPA after his freshman year. That single D acts as a drag on Noah's overall GPA. Noah has dug himself a hole, and climbing out of it will take at least his entire freshman year at State University—if not longer.

Alarmed? You should be. This example shows what happens to a student with a single poor grade. What's more, very few college students make straight As; you'll likely have grades lower than that in your GPA mix. If that's the case, a single poor grade becomes even more of a drag on your GPA.

When you select your courses, never lose sight of how even a single bad grade can affect your GPA. Whenever feasible, take steps to avoid courses that pose a significant risk to your GPA.

University Grade Replacement Policies

Public universities are fully aware of how a couple of low course grades hurt students' GPAs and in turn limit their job and graduate school prospects. In response, many universities have adopted policies to mitigate the damage. Under these policies, often called **grade replacement policies**, a student can repeat a course in which he earns a low grade (often anything below a C), and the university will substitute the new grade for the original one when it calculates the student's institutional GPA.

At first glance, grade replacement may strike you as a heaven-sent second chance. And for college students who are weaker academically, it can be. However, if you hope to graduate on time, with GPA-based honors, and with a broad range of job and graduate school opportunities open to you, these policies won't likely help you, for several reasons.

For starters, although the new grade replaces the original grade in calculating your institutional GPA, the original grade doesn't disappear. At most universities, both grades remain on your transcript. Whenever you provide your transcript to potential employers or graduate school admissions offices, they can usually see both grades and that you took the course a second time.

Further, the original grade doesn't actually get excluded from every calculation of your GPA. For example, most universities count both grades when they determine which students receive GPA-based honors at graduation. This is only fair: students who repeat courses shouldn't have an advantage over those who didn't need a second chance.

Grade replacement policies might not improve your graduate school prospects, either. Many graduate school admissions offices include both the original and the replacement grades when they calculate your cumulative GPA.

Moreover, repeating a course can easily wreck your plan to graduate on time. Many schools don't offer every course every semester, and even if they do, there's no guarantee that space will be available when you try to register. As a result, you may have to wait multiple semesters before you can retake a course. Not surprisingly, this can throw your entire graduation timetable out of whack. Furthermore, when you repeat a course instead of taking a new class that fulfills a degree requirement, it doesn't move you any closer to graduation.

Even if your university has a grade replacement policy, you should always assume every grade you earn will stay with you permanently. Repeating a course is not like hitting the reset button; on the contrary, it can have far-reaching consequences. That's why you should always go into a course with the mindset of doing your best the first time you take it.

Your College GPA and the Big Picture

This Chapter Covers

- How a high GPA can open doors before and after graduation
- Grade inflation and what it means for you

The grades you earn in high school play a big—often the biggest—role in determining which colleges admit you. But the grades you earn in college will likely have a larger impact on your future than your high school grades ever did. In fact, most employers and graduate schools won't look at your high school grades once you have a college degree.

Although your university GPA can have a huge impact on your future, neither high schools nor colleges talk much about that fact. This is understandable. After all, not everyone will be a stellar college student, so it's an uncomfortable and stressful topic.

As a result, however, you may not fully understand exactly why having good grades and a high GPA can be so pivotal, both during and after college. So let's look at some reasons you need to be concerned about your college grades and strive to maximize your GPA.

Your Opportunities On and Off Campus

Good grades and a high GPA don't just affect your plans for after graduation. They can have a big impact on the quality of your overall college experience from the minute you set foot on campus.

Students who get off to a poor start in college sometimes never recover. As we saw in the story about Tyler and Mason in the Introduction, a few low grades during freshman year can put students in a hole from which they never dig out. They spend their remaining years on campus working harder than ever trying to improve their GPA—to the detriment of other aspects of college. They limit their participation in extracurricular activities, and they don't enjoy an active social life.

All too commonly, students with low GPAs aren't happy. Academic woes are the leading cause of unhappiness in college, according to one prominent psychiatrist who specializes in student issues.[13] And those students' parents—who are often footing the bill—aren't happy with the results, either. It's easy to see how academic floundering often leads to friction between students and their parents.

By contrast, students who maintain a high GPA starting from their very first semester put themselves in an excellent position to take advantage of everything college has to offer. A high GPA enables many students to enjoy a higher-quality education than their peers at the same school. At many public universities, for example, only high-GPA students are eligible to participate in university honors programs, which typically offer the finest education available at those campuses. The benefits of these programs may include access to small honors sections of courses taught by top professors, an opportunity to write an honors thesis, and the chance to work on research projects with esteemed faculty members.

Students with a high GPA enjoy a better college experience outside the classroom as well. Because they don't have to work overtime to raise a low GPA, they have more time for extracurricular and social activities. They're able to strike a much better balance between studying and other aspects of college life. And parents are usually more content when their kids have the academic side of college under control.

Don't underestimate the importance of having a life outside of class. Spending time socializing and participating in extracurricular activities can lead to more than just good memories. Today, more than ever, your activities outside the classroom can be critical to positioning you for the future you want. A college education is far more than what you learn from your coursework. Well-chosen activities on and off campus offer an enormous opportunity to gain valuable experience, develop important life skills, and build a network of contacts.

For many students, those experiences, skills, and networks prove far more valuable over the long term than the material they learned in any college classroom. An aspiring journalist might work on the campus newspaper. A future trial lawyer might hone her public speaking skills as a member of the debate team. Another student might pursue an internship that provides valuable work experience and even leads to a job after graduation. Yet another student could use time outside the classroom to launch a startup business venture. The possibilities are endless.

The relationships that well-chosen activities nurture can prove fruitful over the long term. The connections you make through fraternities and sororities, professional organizations, sports teams, and other activities on and off campus often pay big dividends later. No matter how well you do in college, you'll likely need someone to help open doors for you in the job market. The more extensive and developed your network of contacts, the more you can leverage that network after graduation.

It is possible, of course, to develop your abilities and skills as well as professional and social networks without maintaining a high GPA. But in today's competitive world, students who are able to combine a high GPA with those other elements will have a big advantage.

Your Career

Getting That First Job Out of College

You've probably already heard that finding a decent job once you graduate from college can be tough. In fact, today more than half of all bachelor's degree holders under the age of 25 are jobless or underemployed.[14] But your situation may be even tougher, because you probably don't want just any old job. You want the right first job, the one with a highly regarded employer in a field that interests you, gets your career off to a great start, and offers the work-life balance you seek. Competition for those highly desirable jobs is fierce; the number of qualified applicants far exceeds the number of available positions. That leaves employers in the driver's seat, allowing them to be very selective when they interview for open positions.

More than 73 percent of employers say that they have screened job candidates by GPA, according to a report by the National Association of Colleges and Employers.[15] Because there are so many job-seekers for so few positions, many employers won't even interview applicants whose GPA falls below a certain level. They use what is sometimes called a **GPA hurdle rate** to screen potential college hires. If your GPA doesn't clear the hurdle, you won't even get an interview.

Sometimes universities will set their own GPA hurdle rates for on-campus interviews, to help screen out students they think will make unqualified or unimpressive candidates. Just as students compete for jobs, universities compete with one another to lure companies to visit campus and interview their students. They want employers to return every year and to hire their graduates. This gives universities a big incentive to put their best face forward—by showcasing students with impressive GPAs.

What does this mean for you? It often means that only the students with the highest GPAs get interviews for the most desirable jobs. Their high GPAs can, almost literally, open doors. Conversely, students with average or low GPAs never even get invited to interview with many companies. They don't even get a foot in the door.

Your Long-Term Earnings Potential

You shouldn't assume that a high GPA is useful only for landing you that first job out of college or getting you into graduate school. It may also have a long-term impact on your career and earnings potential. There is a large and significant relationship between college GPA and future earnings, according to one study. A one-point increase in a student's GPA correlates with a nine percent increase in earnings 10 years after graduation.[16] That can add up to an enormous amount of money over your career.

Your Graduate School Prospects

For many of you, your undergraduate degree won't be your last university degree. A graduate degree is a prerequisite for many careers and desirable for others. If you hope to attend a highly regarded graduate school of any kind—law, medicine, business, or any other field—you want a strong undergraduate GPA to bolster your chances.

Don't take our word for it. Find out the average undergraduate GPA of the students who attend leading graduate schools in a field that interests you. You may be surprised at how high a GPA you need to make yourself a realistic contender for admission. This will also give you an idea of what you're working toward, and why it's so important to have a strategy now to maintain a GPA that keeps your choice of graduate schools within reach.

Other Factors

Many of you already understand that a high GPA can open important doors for you. But there are some less obvious reasons a high GPA is more critical than you might think.

Private University Students Have Significantly Higher GPAs Than Public University Students

Typically, GPAs at private universities are higher than those at public universities. One extensive study of undergraduate GPAs found that at private universities, the average GPA is around 3.3, while the average at public universities is around 3.0.[17]

What does this mean for you? Public university students are at a disadvantage compared to private university students, even before you consider other advantages private university students may have. Private university students are competing with you for jobs and graduate school admission. Their higher GPAs can easily make them appear more qualified than graduates of public universities with similar class ranks. This explains, in part, why private university students are overrepresented in leading graduate school programs.

Again, this may not seem fair, but it's a fact of life. You're competing with a lot of other students for jobs, spots in graduate school programs, and other potential opportunities. And not just with students from your university, but from every other one as well. You need to recognize this and develop your own strategy to achieve a GPA that will open doors to the future you want.

Grade Inflation

The prevalence today of **grade inflation**—the process by which student grades have gradually edged higher over time—makes a high overall GPA even more important to your future. Over the last several decades, grades at public universities have risen considerably, causing overall GPAs to rise as well. For example, at the University of Florida, the state's flagship public university, the average GPA of undergraduate students rose from 3.0 in fall 1997 to 3.3 in spring 2009.[18]

Are students today really that much smarter? Who knows! Grades are on the rise at many public universities for a number of reasons, and they're hotly disputed. Whatever the reason, your first instinct might be to think that grade inflation is a good thing for you. After all, it could mean that your grades and GPA may be somewhat higher than they would have been if you'd attended college a decade or two ago.

But in reality, grade inflation isn't good for you. Grade inflation doesn't just raise your GPA; it raises everyone's. The fact that GPAs are much higher today than ever before makes it all the more important for you to have the highest one possible. You'll need higher grades in order to stand out from your peers. Don't fool yourself into thinking a 3.0, or B average, is a "good" GPA. At many public universities today, a 3.0 GPA is actually below average.

Keep grade inflation in mind when you think about the grades you want. This may keep you motivated to develop a strategy that helps ensure that you maintain a GPA that positively differentiates you from the masses of other students.

Making the Grade: What You Should Know About University Grading Practices

This Chapter Covers

- Curved and criteria-based grading
- Weed-out courses

Imagine you have a choice when you select your courses: you can take a course in which only a small set of students—say, 15 percent—can ever get an A, no matter how well they learn the material and demonstrate that they know it on exams. Or you can select the same course, taught by a different professor, in which all the students whose work in the course merits an A will get one. All other things being equal, you'd take the course where you get the A if the work you do deserves one, wouldn't you?

Seems obvious, right?

Unfortunately, many new students don't pay any attention to how their courses are graded. This isn't because they can't find out the information; it's often readily available or even provided to them. Rather, they don't pay attention because they begin college without understanding the fundamental ways in which college-level grading differs from high school.

Don't be one of those students. You need to understand how grading at the university level works before you select your first-semester courses.

This chapter introduces two fundamental approaches to university grading: curved and criteria-based grading. We also discuss weed-out courses, slang for college courses (often introductory-level offerings) that are designed to flunk the weakest students, or at least discourage them from further study in that subject. Once you understand the very different ways your instructors can grade you, you can put this information to work when you design your university game plan and choose your courses and instructors.

Grading on the Curve

Many university courses and instructors use a rank-based grading commonly known as "grading on the curve," or **curved grading**.

Despite the widespread use of curved grading, many students don't understand exactly how it works. Simply put, it means that students receive a grade based not on their demonstrated mastery of the material, but rather on how they score compared to the other students in that course.

If you haven't started college yet, the closest thing you may have experienced to curved grading is the percentile rank you received on a standardized test given to all high school students in your state. In those exams, you didn't receive a score based strictly on your knowledge of the material tested. Rather, your score placed you somewhere among all the students who took the exam. If you placed within the 80th percentile in reading, for example, you scored higher than 80 percent of the people who took the test at the same time you did. Your percentile rank depended not on how many questions you answered correctly, but on how well you scored relative to all the other test-takers.

Curved grading works in much the same way. You receive a numerical score based on how well you complete the required coursework. All the students in your class are then ranked by their numerical scores and divided into percentiles. Your actual grade depends on your percentile, or how you rank compared to all the other students in the class.

There's no uniform method for grading on a curve. The percentiles may be determined by university policies or by the individual instructors. They can vary widely. For example, in some courses with curved grading, the top 15 percent of students might receive an A, 35 percent a B, 35 percent a C, 10 percent a D, and the remaining 5 percent an F. The illustration below shows this grade distribution:

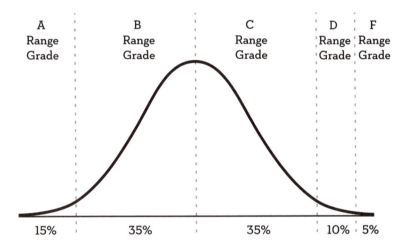

A Range Grade	B Range Grade	C Range Grade	D Range Grade	F Range Grade
15%	35%	35%	10%	5%

Curved grading transforms classmates into competitors. Instead of earning a grade based solely on how well you demonstrate your understanding of the course material, you get ranked on how well you perform in comparison with the other students sitting in class with you. The result: the more students who "get it," the worse it can be for you. If the guy next to you does worse than you do, that helps you. If he does better, it can result in a lower grade for you.

Whether curved grading helps or hurts you depends on the course. In some cases, a curve hurts because it limits the number of As a professor awards, no matter how many students ace the material. So, for example, even if you maintain a 95 average on your course assignments, you might earn only a B if 20 percent of your classmates score higher than a 95. Your grade depends on how your classmates fare rather than strictly on your performance.

In other cases, a curve can work in your favor. This is especially common in introductory-level STEM (science, technology, engineering, and math) courses, which, by their nature, teach difficult content. Your performance in one of these classes might in reality be equivalent to a C, but you could wind up with a B if most of your classmates perform worse than you do. And if you're good at one of these difficult courses, you might not need to ace the material to get an A; you might only have to perform better than 85 percent of your classmates.

The shape of the curve can also affect your grade. If a professor awards As to the top 20 percent of the class, your chances are better than if she gives As only to the top 10 percent.

The critical things for you to find out are which courses have curves, and what those curves look like. Sometimes, before a course starts, the professor may disclose his intention to grade on a curve and reveal the exact breakdown of final grades. At other times, you'll have to look at how the professor has graded the course in the past to get an idea of what to expect.

Once you have some idea of what the curve in a course may look like, you can decide for yourself if that course makes sense for you. In many cases, when a course will be graded on a harsh curve, you'll want to find a way to fulfill that degree requirement that is less risky to your institutional GPA.

Criteria-Based Grading

Not all college courses get graded on a curve. In many courses, your final grade depends on the extent to which you meet your instructor's expectations for the students in that course, not on how well you do relative to other students. This is sometimes referred to as **criteria-based grading**. At least in theory, under criteria-based grading, all the students in a class could earn an A if they meet the professor's expectations.

From the point of view of your grades, criteria-based grading can be an advantage or a disadvantage. Let's look first at when it can be a disadvantage.

Drill Sergeant Grading

Unfortunately, criteria-based grading can sometimes be more draconian than curved grading. Why? A phenomenon we call **drill sergeant grading**. In these courses, the bar is high, with a lot demanded of students. And when students don't meet expectations, a disproportionately high percentage of low course grades is often the result.

Drill sergeant grading in a course can occur for multiple reasons. Sometimes the course material is very difficult; sometimes students lack the background to tackle the material successfully. At other times, a particular instructor has unreasonably high expectations of what constitutes A-level work. In that last case, you could demonstrate mastery of the material to a degree that other instructors would consider to be A-level, but the drill sergeant gives a lower grade because of his own—often unrealistic—expectations.

Whatever the reason, if you hope to maintain a high GPA, avoiding drill sergeant instructors is a smart strategy.

Measured Grading

Criteria-based grading can also work to your advantage. Most instructors grade in a much more measured manner than their drill sergeant counterparts. **Measured grading** occurs in courses where the instructors set more reasonable expectations for students to meet in order to earn a good grade.

Measured graders may award a disproportionately large percentage of high grades. This doesn't mean their courses are easy. A class can still require a lot of work. The important thing to remember is that in a measured grader's class, you get a final grade—hopefully a high one—that reflects your performance. If you demonstrate a good grasp of the material and meet the instructor's reasonable expectations, your grade will reflect it. You often have more control with this kind of instructor than you do in a course graded on a curve or by a drill sergeant.

Weed-Out Courses

Many courses, whether they have curved or drill sergeant grading (or both), are also **weed-out**, or **weeder, courses**. In these courses, instructors set high hurdles for students, with the expectation—or even the intention—that a significant number of students will receive low grades. Weed-out courses get their name from what people do when they rip out weeds that don't belong in their gardens. In a weed-out course, poorly performing students are the weeds.

Weed-out courses are a handy, if unpleasant, tool universities use to reduce student numbers by thinning the pack. First, they cull students the faculty feels are academically unsuited to the university and probably shouldn't have been admitted in the first place. Second, they dissuade students from pursuing further studies in particular subject areas. The assumption is that after a little weeding, only the students with aptitude in a field will choose to continue in that major. And nothing acts as a bigger deterrent to studying a subject than receiving a C, D, or F in an introductory course.

Cruel? Absolutely. But very effective for universities.

Think of weed-out courses as a form of Darwinism in the university classroom. At some universities, some of the most difficult weed-out courses see student failure rates of around 50 percent every semester.[19] Most weed-out courses aren't that brutal, but they're all designed to be demanding. Coupled with the fact that these courses are often graded on a curve, it can be extremely difficult to get high grades in them, no matter how much effort you make.

What the Different Approaches to Grading Mean for You

The different ways in which university instructors grade their students have big implications for you. In many instances, the grade you earn in a college course won't necessarily reflect your actual performance or your demonstrated mastery of the material. It will also depend on how the course gets graded. Different instructors can award very different grades for exactly the same level and quality of work, so getting a sense of how an instructor generally grades is critical.

Most students don't investigate the grading practices likely to be in use when they choose their courses. Don't make that mistake. Always look before you leap when you select your courses. In Part VI, Learning How to Professor Shop, we'll show you how you can find out how the instructors in your potential courses will likely grade. By doing some detective work beforehand, you can find instructors with grading policies that improve your chances of earning high grades.

6

The GPA Goalpost: Graduating with GPA-Based Honors

This Chapter Covers

- Why you need to know your university's GPA requirements for graduating with honors
- How universities determine GPA-based honors

At this point, you're probably wondering how high a GPA you need to position yourself well for whatever you choose to do once you graduate from college. The answer differs from student to student, so it's something for you to determine. What we can do is give you a sense of the institutional GPA and class standing you need if you want to graduate as a top student. And by top student, we mean in the judgment of public universities themselves: their own requirements to graduate with academic honors based on GPA.

We do this in several ways. First, we explain how public universities award academic honors based on GPA. Then, to give you a sense of the grades you may need to graduate with GPA-based honors, we list the GPAs that 20 public universities around the country required in 2014. Some determine honors based on a set level of institutional GPA, while others determine it through a student's graduating class rank.

Public universities vary in their GPA cutoffs to graduate with the different levels of academic honors. You may be surprised at how high an institutional GPA and class rank students need at some universities, and at how significantly the GPA cutoffs vary from one university to the next. That's exactly why we present so many examples.

By showing you various universities' GPA cutoffs, we want to motivate you to find out on your own where the GPA goalpost to graduate with honors lies at your university. Once you do that, you can begin working toward that goal.

Why You Need to Know Where Your University's GPA Goalpost Sits

All too often, students don't bother to find out the GPA they will need to graduate with GPA-based honors. They just roll along through their studies, often with a low-3-point-something GPA. All the while, they think they're good students, when, in fact, they're completely average. This delusion usually continues for the first few years of college, until students finally start to focus on what they'll do after graduation. They start looking into the average GPAs of the students who typically get hired for the jobs they want, or admitted by the graduate schools they hope to attend, and get smacked down to earth.

Don't become one of those students. In a football game, you don't try to kick a field goal with your eyes closed. You need to know where the goalpost lies before you make your attempt. The same thing goes for your GPA. You need an idea of how high your final GPA must be to graduate with honors so you know what you need to accomplish.

Graduation with GPA-Based Honors

Nearly all public universities recognize the all-star performance of their strongest students by bestowing academic honors on them when they graduate. These honors can be based strictly on a student's GPA, on the completion of specific requirements like an honors program or honors thesis, or on some combination of GPA and the completion of certain courses or other prerequisites. To keep our discussion manageable, we focus on academic honors based strictly on GPA.

The majority of public universities base the cutoff for honors eligibility solely on a student's institutional GPA. Others give some weight to a student's cumulative GPA. (See Chapter 3 for an explanation of these terms.) There's no universal method or cutoff, so be sure you find out your university's approach.

Public universities use different designations for types of academic honors. Many bestow what are known as Latin honors, with three levels, each with its own GPA cutoff or class rank requirement, or a combination of both. They are:

- **Summa cum laude:** the highest designation
- **Magna cum laude:** the middle designation
- **Cum laude:** the lowest designation, but still given to relatively few students

Other public universities use honors designations such as With Distinction, With High Distinction, and With Highest Distinction. Again, each is based on a certain GPA cutoff, class rank, or some combination. Your university may use Honors, High Honors, and Highest Honors. The titles of these GPA-based honors vary, but no matter the name, they all require good grades.

The level of GPA a student needs to graduate with GPA-based honors also differs from one university to another, although it's usually high. In general, public universities determine eligibility for GPA-based honors in one of two ways:

GPA-Based Honors Determined Through a Strict GPA Cutoff

All students with a GPA at or above a specific cutoff receive the level of honors their GPA warrants. These universities place no limit on the number of students who can graduate with these honors.

GPA-Based Honors Determined Through Class Rank

At these universities, class rank—either in the entire graduating class or within a specific college—determines who graduates with honors. Sometimes honors are based on the GPA of current students compared to that of students in previous classes, which makes it only a rough approximation of a student's actual class rank. Under this system, a university bestows its highest GPA-based honors on the graduating students whose GPAs fall within the highest band of a certain percentile ranking, the next level on students whose GPAs fall within a somewhat lower percentile ranking, and so on.

If your university determines honors this way, you may not know the exact GPA threshold you need in order to be eligible; you may only know the class rank you must attain to qualify.

Some Examples

At GPAMaxx, we believe that far too few students know where the GPA goalpost at their own university lies. They don't have any idea what final institutional GPA they will need to graduate with honors. We think that if more students knew this, it would shake up their undergraduate game plan and make them focus more on their grades and GPA.

To give you a sense of the level of institutional GPA you may need to graduate with GPA-based honors, we set out below the requirements at 20 public universities around the United States. The information compiled here is accurate through 2014. All of these universities have a maximum final institutional GPA of 4.0. The first 10 universities determine eligibility for GPA-based honors strictly on GPA; the next 10 use a student's rank in his or her own class or measured against one or more previous graduating classes.

GPA-Based Honors Determined Strictly Through an Institutional GPA Cutoff

The table for each of the 10 universities below sets forth the name and level of the honor on the left, and the minimum institutional GPA students needed for each level on the right.

Arizona State University

Type of GPA-based honors	Minimum institutional GPA required
Summa cum laude	3.8
Magna cum laude	3.6
Cum laude	3.4

Auburn University (Alabama)

Type of GPA-based honors	Minimum institutional GPA required
Summa cum laude	3.8
Magna cum laude	3.6
Cum laude	3.4

Binghamton University, The State University of New York

Type of GPA-based honors	Minimum institutional GPA required
Summa cum laude	3.85
Magna cum laude	3.7
Cum laude	3.5

Florida International University

Type of GPA-based honors	Minimum institutional GPA required
Summa cum laude	3.9
Magna cum laude	3.7
Cum laude	3.5

George Mason University (Virginia)

Type of GPA-based honors	Minimum institutional GPA required
Summa cum laude	3.9
Magna cum laude	3.7
Cum laude	3.5

Kansas State University

Type of GPA-based honors	Minimum institutional GPA required
Summa cum laude	3.95
Magna cum laude	3.85
Cum laude	3.75

Texas A&M University

Type of GPA-based honors	Minimum institutional GPA required
Summa cum laude	3.9
Magna cum laude	3.7
Cum laude	3.5

University of Maine

Type of GPA-based honors	Minimum institutional GPA required
Summa cum laude	3.7
Magna cum laude	3.5
Cum laude	3.3

University of North Carolina at Chapel Hill

Type of GPA-based honors	Minimum institutional GPA required
With Highest Distinction	3.8
With Distinction	3.5

University of North Dakota

Type of GPA-based honors	Minimum institutional GPA required
Summa cum laude	3.9
Magna cum laude	3.7
Cum laude	3.5

GPA-Based Honors Determined Through Class Rank

The first column lists the name and level of GPA-based honors, the second the percentile rank in a student's graduating class, and the third the minimum institutional GPA required. Where applicable, we indicate when the university bestows GPA-based honors based on a student's rank among graduates of his or her individual college, rather than the entire university.

Colorado State University, Fort Collins

Type of GPA-based honors	% rank in graduating class of particular college at university	Minimum institutional GPA required in the College of Liberal Arts
Summa cum laude	Top 1%	3.96
Magna cum laude	Next 3%	3.87
Cum laude	Next 6%	3.70

Michigan State University

Type of GPA-based honors	% rank in graduating class	Minimum institutional GPA required
With High Honor	Top 6%	3.87
With Honor	Next 14%	3.69

Northern Arizona University

Type of GPA-based honors	% rank in graduating class of particular college at university	Minimum institutional GPA required in the College of Arts & Letters
Summa cum laude	Top 5%	3.97
Magna cum laude	Next 5%	3.91
Cum laude	Next 10%	3.81

Temple University (Pennsylvania)

Type of GPA-based honors	% rank in graduating class of particular college at university	Minimum institutional GPA required in the College of Liberal Arts
Summa cum laude	Top 2%	3.94
Magna cum laude	Next 5%	3.82
Cum laude	Next 9%	3.67

University of California, Santa Barbara

Type of GPA-based honors	% rank in graduating class of particular college at university	Minimum institutional GPA required in the College of Letters & Science
Highest Honors	Top 2.5%	3.89
High Honors	Next 6%	3.73
Honors	Next 11.5%	3.54

University of Connecticut, Storrs

Type of GPA-based honors	% rank in graduating class of particular college at university	Minimum institutional GPA required in the College of Liberal Arts & Sciences
Summa cum laude	Top 5%	3.896
Magna cum laude	Next 10%	3.727
Cum laude	Next 10%	3.578

University of Texas at Austin

Type of GPA-based honors	% rank in graduating class of particular college at university	Minimum institutional GPA required in the College of Liberal Arts
Highest Honors	Top 4%	3.929
High Honors	Next 6%	3.844
Honors	Next 10%	3.695

University of Utah

Type of GPA-based honors	% rank in graduating class of particular college at university	Minimum institutional GPA required in the College of Humanities
Summa cum laude	Top 1%	3.981
Magna cum laude	Next 2.5%	3.926
Cum laude	Next 4.5%	3.841

University of Washington, Seattle

Type of GPA-based honors	% rank in graduating class of particular college at university	Minimum institutional GPA required in the College of Arts & Sciences
Summa cum laude	Top 0.5%	3.96
Magna cum laude	Next 3%	3.86
Cum laude	Next 6.5%	3.75

University of Wyoming

Type of GPA-based honors	% rank in graduating class of particular college at university	Minimum institutional GPA required in the College of Arts & Sciences
Summa cum laude	Top 1%	4.0
Magna cum laude	Next 4%	3.941
Cum laude	Next 5%	3.843

Were you surprised by the GPAs needed to graduate with honors at these universities? Though they vary, they all have one thing in common: you need a good GPA to graduate with any type of GPA-based honors. Even at the universities with lower cutoffs, students need solid GPAs to qualify for honors.

Obviously, graduating with any type of GPA-based honors takes a lot of hard work. But for most college students, hard work isn't enough. That's why having a university game plan and knowing how to pick courses conducive to your success in them are so important. Be sure to look where your university sets its GPA goalpost. You may not like where it sits, but you need to know so you can set your own goal to graduate with the highest level of GPA-based honors that you can.

Getting to Know Your University Road Map

Too many college students make the strategic error of not fully understanding the course requirements they have to fulfill in order to graduate, and the options they have to satisfy those requirements. The main problem: they don't bother really getting to know their degree plan, the road map to their university graduation. In Part III, we provide the background you need to get to know your degree plan in depth.

After reading Part III, you'll better understand the structure of your degree plan and the different types of coursework you must complete to obtain your degree.

Know Your University Road Map—Your Degree Plan: GPAMaxx Cardinal Rule #1

This Chapter Covers

- Your degree plan as a road map
- A sample public university degree plan
- Fundamental blunders that students often make because they don't understand their degree plans

Your **degree plan** is the document that sets forth all the course requirements you must fulfill in order to graduate from your university. But it's more than that. A degree plan is essentially your university road map. If you follow it, it will lead you to graduation.

Even if you have a road map, though, there's often more than one way to reach your destination. You want to understand all the roads available to you so that you can plot out your optimal route. It's the same with your degree plan. You want to complete your college journey in the way that produces optimal results for you and best positions you for success afterward.

The principle behind GPAMaxx Cardinal Rule #1 is simple: to maximize your academic success and graduate on time, you must thoroughly understand the requirements of your university degree plan and the various ways you can fulfill them.

A Sample Degree Plan

Because many of you have never seen a degree plan, here is a sample that lists the course and other requirements for a management major seeking a Bachelor of Business Administration (B.B.A.) degree:

State University
College of Business Administration
MANAGEMENT B.B.A.

2014–17 DEGREE PLAN

General Education Requirements

WRITTEN & ORAL LITERACY (each of the following)	HUMANITIES (1 of the following)
☐ ENG 301 Composition I ☐ SPE 301 Interpersonal Communication	☐ ARH 306 History of Western Art ☐ PHL 310 Intro to Ethics ☐ ENG 316 World Literature ☐ ANT 305 Intro to Folklore

MATHEMATICS (1 of each of the following)	WORLD HISTORY (1 of the following)
☐ MTH 405 Differential & Integral Calculus I ☐ MTH 403 Business Calculus I and ☐ MTH 406 Differential & Integral Calculus II ☐ MTH 404 Business Calculus II	☐ HIS 301 History of Western Civilization to 1648 ☐ HIS 302 History of Western Civilization from 1648 ☐ HIS 305 Survey of World History

LAB SCIENCES (3 of the following)	AMERICAN TRADITIONS (2 of the following)
☐ ANT 301 Intro to Physical Anthropology ☐ AST 301 Intro to Astronomy ☐ BIO 401 Intro to Biology ☐ CHE 401 Intro to Chemistry ☐ ENV 302 Environmental Science ☐ GEO 401 Physical Geology	☐ GOV 310 American National Government ☐ HIS 311 U.S. History to 1865 ☐ HIS 312 U.S. History since 1865 ☐ HIS 315 Mexican-American History ☐ HIS 317 African-American History

VISUAL & PERFORMING ARTS (1 of the following)	SOCIAL AWARENESS (1 of the following)
☐ ARC 305 Architecture & Society ☐ MUS 301 Intro to Music ☐ THE 303 Intro to Theatre & Dance	☐ PSY 301 Intro to Psychology ☐ SOC 301 Intro to Sociology ☐ GRG 302 Human & Cultural Geography ☐ ANT 302 Intro to Cultural Anthropology ☐ GNS 301 Intro to Gender Studies ☐ COM 304 Mass Media & Society

Major Requirements	
LOWER-DIVISION BUSINESS CORE	UPPER-DIVISION BUSINESS CORE
☐ ECO 301 Principles of Microeconomics ☐ ECO 302 Principles of Macroeconomics ☐ ACC 310 Fundamentals of Financial Accounting ☐ ACC 311 Fundamentals of Managerial Accounting ☐ BUS 310 Legal Environment of Business ☐ MIS 301 Intro to Management Information Systems ☐ STA 305 Fundamentals of Business Statistics	☐ BUS 325 Oral & Written Business Communication ☐ MKT 320 Principles of Marketing ☐ MAN 325 Organizational Behavior ☐ FIN 335 Principles of Business Finance
MAJOR CORE	

☐ MAN 320 Principles of Management
☐ MAN 330 Human Resource Management
☐ MAN 350 Operations & Supply Chain Management
☐ MAN 360 Strategic Management
	☐ MAN 372 Topics in Management (3 of the following)
	   ☐ The Art & Science of Negotiation
	   ☐ Management in the Cross-Border Context
	   ☐ Leadership Issues
	   ☐ Groups & Teams
	   ☐ Industrial Relations

Minor Requirements
Twelve hours in single field approved by departmental academic advisor with at least nine hours being upper division. ☐ _____   ☐ _____   ☐ _____   ☐ _____

Electives
Additional hours as needed to complete the minimum 120 hours required for B.B.A. and upper division and in residence hours (see checklist below).

General Degree Requirements Checklist	
☐ A minimum of 120 hours total ☐ 42 hours upper division (24 hours upper division in residence) ☐ 60 hours in residence (not credit by examination or correspondence) ☐ 33 hours of major and 6 hours of minor in residence ☐ 24 of last 30 hours in residence ☐ 45 hours maximum credit by examination	☐ No more than 36 hours in one subject ☐ No more than 36 hours in one college (except College of Business Administration) ☐ No more than 13 hours pass/fail (only electives may be taken pass/fail) ☐ State University GPA of 2.0 in all courses attempted ☐ State University GPA of 2.0 in major and minor

Notes

Bear in mind that universities and their departments lay out degree plans very differently from one another, so the one at your university might not look like this. Some universities' degree plans are far less detailed. Unfortunately, many universities don't list all the course requirements that students must complete on the degree plan itself. If you study at one of those universities, you may have to pull together the information on your own so you can view your requirements all at once.

Students and Their Degree Plans: Potential Fundamental Blunders

When students don't get to know their degree plans, they often make two fundamental strategic blunders.

BLUNDER #1

Students don't understand even the most basic requirements of their degree plan and, as a result, fail to graduate on time—or at all

Maybe they don't have a copy of the degree plan. Maybe they have a copy but haven't paid much attention to it. In either case, a lack of familiarity with their degree plan leads to the same blunder: students take courses that don't satisfy requirements toward their degree, and they neglect to take courses they need to graduate. That can delay their graduation by a semester, a year, or more. All too often, failing to understand the requirements of their degree plan prevents students from graduating at all.

These mistakes cost students both time and money. As we discussed at the end of Chapter 1, when students don't graduate on time, they pay for it. Not only do they fork over additional tuition dollars to their university, they also miss out on tens of thousands of dollars in lost wages by delaying their entry into the workforce. Taken together, these amounts can easily equal the cost of a new car or even a down payment on a house. That's big money!

BLUNDER #2

Students have a basic awareness of their degree plan's requirements but don't understand them well enough to fulfill them in the most suitable and GPA-friendly way

The majority of university students make this mistake. They take courses that fulfill degree plan requirements but that aren't a good fit for other reasons. Because they haven't made the effort to understand the full range of course choices they have and the different ways they can fulfill them, students make strategic errors that hurt their grades and keep them from maximizing their academic potential. Students fall victim to this blunder because they don't understand what's permitted under their degree plans.

For example, students take courses in subjects poorly suited to their individual strengths or that they simply don't like. Often, they make these mistakes even though they could have fulfilled the same requirements with better-fitting courses. Or they complete courses in their worst subjects at their own universities, where their grades in those courses negatively affect their institutional GPA, instead of fulfilling those course requirements in a way that has no impact on their institutional GPA.

The most unfortunate thing about each of these blunders is that they're often preventable. It doesn't take a lot of effort to avoid these pitfalls, but countless students fall victim to them every semester because they don't have a university game plan or a strategy.

Don't make those mistakes. Get to know your university road map: your degree plan.

A Study in Contrasts: Students Who Know Their Degree Plan

In stark contrast to students who don't know or are only vaguely familiar with their degree plan are students who understand it well and use that knowledge to their strategic advantage. Those students are empowered. If you thoroughly understand the requirements of your degree plan, you can:

- Be proactive in managing your college career. Rather than allowing your degree plan's requirements to control you, you can be in command.

- Choose the courses you take to complete your degree and simultaneously maintain a high GPA by carefully selecting your courses, instructors, and even course formats.

- Take courses you're interested in that both satisfy your degree plan requirements and offer you the best chances for high grades.

- Identify potentially difficult course requirements of your degree plan and create a plan to maneuver around them with your GPA intact. You can often find creative ways to minimize the impact of courses that pose a real threat to your institutional GPA.

- Develop and regularly update your game plan to fulfill your degree plan requirements on time (or even early).

- Minimize the risk of receiving bad advice from your university academic advisor. When you know what you need to do to graduate and the different ways to get there, you're in a better position to discuss your university career and course selections with your advisor.

- Eliminate the temptation to take classes because everyone else is. Make informed decisions regarding the best courses for you rather than following the crowd.

- Plan your coursework to allow a healthy balance of academic, extracurricular, and social activities.

When it comes to your degree plan, knowledge really is power.

Despite all the advantages that come from knowing your degree plan, you'd be shocked at how few university students empower themselves with a thorough understanding of their own. It takes some time to get to know your degree plan, but that time can pay big dividends in the form of more suitable and enjoyable courses, better grades, a higher GPA, more time for important things outside of class, and an on-time (or even early) graduation. Always keep this first GPAMaxx Cardinal Rule front and center as you decide how to fulfill your degree plan requirements.

What a Degree Plan Really Is: A Contract

While it's helpful to think of a degree plan as a road map, you should also consider it a contract between you and your university.

In a degree plan, your university establishes the contractual terms, consisting of the course and credit hour requirements you must satisfy, along with the conditions and limitations on how you may fulfill these obligations. Once you satisfy all the contractual requirements of your degree plan, you have fulfilled your end of the bargain, and the university is obligated to award you a degree.

As with any other contract, you want to derive the greatest possible benefits from it. Ideally, you want to fulfill the contract in the way that benefits you most: by getting stellar grades to increase the likelihood that you'll have great career, graduate school, and other opportunities when you graduate, and to graduate on time or even early. You also want to get your degree cost-effectively, while still enjoying the extracurricular and social activities that can result in lifelong friendships and valuable business and social connections. As you fulfill your requirements toward your university degree, always remember that you are satisfying your end of a contractual bargain. Complete the terms of this contract in the ways that provide you with the most benefits and best further your goals.

8

Dissecting University Degree Plans

This Chapter Covers

- University rules and policies
- Components of degree plans and common pitfalls
- Online coursework

The previous chapter provided you with a basic introduction to the degree plan, the document that sets forth the course requirements you must fulfill in order to graduate. In this chapter, we explore degree plans in greater depth.

Rules and Policies Governing Degree Plans

Your university, your college or school within the university, and the department that houses your major have rules and policies specifying exactly how you may complete the requirements of your degree plan. Among many other things, these detailed rules and policies spell out:

- The number of credit hours you need to graduate

- The number of credit hours you must complete in residence at your university and any exceptions to residency requirements (in study abroad programs, for example)

- The ability to test out of courses entirely through credit by examination (CBE)

- The permissibility of taking courses at other colleges to fulfill degree plan requirements

- Restrictions regarding online coursework

Where to Find Them

You can find the rules and policies that govern your degree plan in various places, depending on which university you attend. Some may appear on your degree plan itself. Others may appear in your university's catalog or bulletin. You may find some or all of them on your university's website, or they may be available only on request. Often, it's some combination of all of these.

The degree of effort needed to find the applicable rules and policies also varies considerably from university to university. Given how important this information is to students, you might think that it would generally be easy to find. Unfortunately, many universities don't place a premium on making this information easily accessible to students. All too often, locating all the information you need can resemble a scavenger hunt, with the relevant rules and policies scattered in a number of places.

Degree Plans Made Easy: Component Coursework

Your degree plan requires you to complete a certain number of courses in order to graduate. Public university degree plans vary enormously depending on what and where you study, but most include three primary types of course requirements:

- General education courses
- Major and minor courses
- Elective courses

General Education Courses

General education course requirements—also commonly referred to as GenEd requirements, core curriculum, liberal arts curriculum, and breadth requirements—refer to coursework required of all students in university degree programs. Typically completed during the first four semesters of college, general education courses usually make up somewhere between a quarter and a third of the total credit hours required to graduate.

Your general education requirements serve as a way for your university to ensure that you receive a multidisciplinary education and a base of knowledge in a variety of academic disciplines. For many university students, these courses also provide the opportunity to investigate subject areas in which they might want to specialize. Many students enter college with no idea of what they'd like to major in. And many who enter with a specific major change their minds after they arrive on campus. By "forcing" them to sample courses in a variety of academic disciplines, universities help students gain a better sense of what they want to study in depth.

In addition to general education requirements, schools or colleges within a university commonly have their own additional core course requirements. For example, the College of Liberal Arts at State University might require its students to complete several semesters of a foreign language, but the College of Engineering would not. Conversely, State University's College of Engineering might require its students to complete an engineering methods course, something the College of Liberal Arts does not.

The number of core course requirements described in the previous paragraph can be sizeable and vary significantly, depending on your major and university. Some of these courses may not officially be a part of your university's general education curriculum, but the issues and pitfalls associated with them are often similar to those of general education courses. For that reason, you should think of them as a sort of general education curriculum within the school or college of your major.

General Education Distribution Requirements

To ensure that students receive a broad-based education, degree plans typically require them to complete general education requirements in a set number of courses across a wide range of academic disciplines, commonly referred to as **distributions**.

Degree plans often permit students to choose general education courses from a list of options within each distribution. It may be helpful to think of these general education requirements as a lengthy menu. You choose one appetizer from a list of starters, one entrée from a list of main courses, one or two side dishes, and a dessert. Distributions function in much the same way: you pick the course or courses you want from each category. Some majors provide students with many course choices to satisfy most distributions, while others are more restrictive. In STEM subjects and some vocational majors, students may have only one or two course choices to satisfy certain distributions.

As an example, at one large public university, the general education distribution requirements for all students consist of the following:

Distribution	Credit Hours Required	Number of Required Courses
Freshman Seminar	3	1
English Composition	3	1
Humanities	3	1
American & State Government	6	2
American History	6	2
Social & Behavioral Sciences	3	1
Mathematics	3	1
Science & Technology	9	3
Visual & Performing Arts	3	1
General Culture	3	1

Because the general education courses in each distribution are usually designed to provide students with an overview of the subject, they're often introductory in nature. These general education courses, as well as others geared primarily toward students in the first two years of their studies, are commonly referred to as **lower-division** courses. The general nature of these courses also means that many other colleges, including community colleges, offer courses covering the same topics that can satisfy general education requirements.

Most public universities permit their students to satisfy many or even all of these requirements by taking the courses at other colleges and then transferring credit for them to their own universities. If that's the case at yours, you have a great deal of flexibility regarding where you actually complete your general education coursework. Even better, you may have the option to test out of many general education courses entirely. Most public universities allow students to take exams covering the material taught in many general education courses, giving you the option to earn credit by examination (CBE) instead.

> You'll find more information about CBE and its potential as a strategic alternative to taking courses at your university in Chapters 9 and 10. Turn to Chapter 11 for more in-depth information about transfer credit and its potential as a strategic alternative to taking courses at your university.

General Education Course Pitfalls

Students can run into a lot of trouble when selecting and completing general education classes. Here are some things that regularly trip students up:

Size Does Matter

General education courses are commonly the most impersonal and intimidating ones university students ever take. Because these courses are required of all students, they are commonly among the largest classes on campus.

Picture this situation: you suddenly find yourself in a giant auditorium, sitting with hundreds of other students, while the instructor lectures with little or no input from you and your classmates. The instructor typically won't know your name, let alone whether you understand the material or need extra help. These **auditorium-size courses**, as we refer to them, are often the norm in general education subjects at public universities.

Sound different from your high school courses? They are. Many new college students have difficulty adjusting because they are accustomed to smaller and more personalized high school classes.

Depending on your major, university classes usually shrink in size and become much more personal and engaging once you get past your introductory and general education courses. In many cases, particularly if you pursue a less common major, those classes can be even more intimate than the ones you had in high school. The trick is to survive the introductory and general education courses with your GPA in good shape.

A Tricky Transition

A related pitfall is the fact that students often take most or all of their general education courses in their first few semesters of college. For many students, this period represents a time of great transition. Most college courses differ enormously from high school classes, requiring students to adapt to unfamiliar styles of instruction and studying.

But that's only one side of the transition. At the same time, many students are living away from home and making decisions without the help of their parents for the first time. Successfully adapting to the different, often heavy demands of college courses while adjusting to the college lifestyle proves tricky for many students. This combination of demands on a student's time and attention can make general education courses especially challenging.

Stringent Grading

Unfortunately, many instructors in general education courses utilize curved and drill sergeant grading, the practices discussed in Chapter 5. Significant numbers of general education courses may also be weed-out courses. As a result, it can be difficult for you to get the grades you want in general education courses, no matter how much effort you put into them.

The fact that many general education courses are harshly graded makes them among the most potentially dangerous ones for you and your GPA. Many very bright students receive their first below-average or even failing grade in a general education course. If you don't select them carefully, general education courses can inflict serious damage on your GPA right at the start of your university career.

Interest Can Be Everything ... Unless You Aren't Particularly Interested

Unlike courses in your major or minor, in which you will hopefully have at least some interest or aptitude, general education courses often cover subjects that you would never study if you weren't required to do so. All too often, general education courses are completely irrelevant to your academic and career goals. You take many of them only to fulfill a distribution requirement, not because they interest you. A physics major with zero interest in art or theater, for example, still may have to complete a course in the visual and performing arts distribution of her degree plan. A history major may have to satisfy a math distribution requirement. It's therefore surprisingly easy to find yourself enrolled in a general education course for which you lack intellectual curiosity or aptitude.

Combine an utter lack of interest with the fact that many general education classes are weed-out courses graded on a harsh curve or taught by drill sergeant instructors, and you can easily find yourself in over your head if you don't select your general education courses carefully.

Major and Minor Courses

The second area of substantial coursework under most degree programs incorporates the areas of study in which you specialize: a major and a minor.

What's a Major, Exactly?

Your **major** is the field of study that's your primary area of specialization. Expect to take more courses in your major than in any single other field.

Your degree plan spells out the requirements for your major, which can vary enormously from one major to another. Most initially require you to complete introductory courses that provide you with a foundation in the discipline. These courses serve as prerequisites for more advanced courses in the field; you must complete them before you take the higher-level ones. Majors sometimes require students in their final year to complete an individual assignment like a thesis or a senior project.

Majors can be organized very differently, depending on what and where you study. Some majors use an extremely structured building-block approach, with each course building on the material taught in a previous course. One course serves as a prerequisite for another course, which in turn serves as a prerequisite for another course, and so on. This is often the case in STEM and certain vocational majors like business administration, nursing, and advertising. In contrast, some other majors can be far less structured, with fewer specific required courses. These majors usually require you to complete a couple of core courses, and then offer you many more options for the rest of your courses and the order in which you take them.

Your Minor

A **minor** is your secondary area of subject specialization. Some degree plans don't require a minor; for those that do, the requirements can vary enormously. Because a minor is only a secondary field of study, it normally involves substantially less coursework than a major.

Requirements of Majors and Minors

The requirements for classes in your major and minor are often stricter than those for your other courses. For example, universities often require students to take many or most of the courses in their major and minor at their university, not at another college. Most degree plans also require students to take at least a majority of the coursework in their major and minor in **upper-division courses**. These classes are often geared primarily toward juniors and seniors, and they often require the completion of introductory classes as a prerequisite.

Pitfalls of Majors and Minors

Students encounter all sorts of problems when they take courses in their major and minor. Here are a few:

Time-Intensive

Since your major is the area in which you specialize, the courses often involve a great deal of work relative to the number of credit hours you receive. This is especially true in upper-division courses, for which you must budget considerable time.

On the plus side, upper-division courses in most majors are not typically weed-out courses, and the grades awarded are often higher than those in general education courses. The tradeoff is that professors demand a lot of their students, so you should plan to devote significant time to these courses.

Few or No Course Choices

In contrast to general education requirements, for which you often have a number of course choices to fulfill each distribution, many majors require the completion of specific courses, some or all of which must be taken at your university. It may be tricky—or even impossible—to find a creative way around taking the most difficult and time-consuming courses required for your major.

In fact, students enrolled in some majors find that there's only a single instructor teaching a required course. That makes it impossible to shop around for the most grade-friendly instructor, or to find a section being taught in a format that fits well with your learning style. You have to take the course at your university with that one instructor—no exceptions.

Selecting a Major for Which You Have Limited Interest or Aptitude

Many students select a major or minor for which they have little interest or aptitude, believing it will provide them with some career advantage after graduation. Maybe their parents want them to be doctors, so they major in biology even though they struggled in high school science classes. Or maybe they've heard that accounting majors have great career prospects, so they major in accounting even though numbers bore them to tears and they hated their high school math classes. We could point to lots of real-life examples.

Unfortunately, things often go badly for students who choose a major for which they lack interest or aptitude. They set themselves up for years of self-inflicted pain and suffering, a surefire recipe for poor grades and a low GPA. If you have little aptitude in a subject, you won't magically become an academic all-star just by majoring in it. Spending the summer before college boning up on the subject probably won't help, either.

Former engineering and science students who switched majors after taking a wrecking ball to their GPAs often resurface in business administration and other nonscientific degree programs. Unfortunately, by the time they switch majors, they've done irreversible damage. Just because they switched doesn't mean the grades in their old majors disappeared; their transcripts and GPAs remain permanently scarred. All too often, these students spend the remainder of their college careers climbing out of the GPA hole they dug by taking engineering and science courses for which they had little aptitude.

Make sure you avoid this trap. You'll likely take more courses in your major than in any other single area. Don't torture yourself by picking a major you won't like or for which you just don't have much aptitude. Odds are you'll be unhappy, and misery doesn't lead to an outstanding GPA.

Elective Courses

The third significant area of required coursework is **electives**, which are the classes you take to round out your education. Most public universities offer a wide range of elective courses. While electives don't usually fulfill any specific course requirements of your degree plan, they still count toward the total number of credit hours you need to graduate. More important, they count toward your GPA, so you want to choose them wisely.

A Pitfall of Elective Courses: Failing to Select Strategically

At many universities, students have almost free rein when it comes to selecting electives. That makes them the wild cards of your degree plan, because they offer excellent opportunities to raise your overall GPA. Unfortunately, many students don't choose their elective courses strategically, and that oversight can come back to haunt them.

As a general rule, you should enroll only in elective courses for which you feel you have a very good chance of earning an A. When chosen wisely, electives can be a virtual bonanza for your GPA. Just be sure not to take elective courses in which your grade could pose even a minimal risk to your GPA.

Seem obvious? Based on what happens to many students, it isn't. They take courses to broaden their education in unfamiliar subjects instead of using the opportunity to boost their GPA through more suitable electives. Not only don't they earn A's, but they have to spend significant time on those courses at the expense of their required ones.

Many universities permit their students to take the equivalent of an entire semester's worth of electives pass/fail. The intent of these policies is to encourage students to broaden their academic horizons by exploring new subjects without fearing a low grade. Taking pass/fail courses may sound appealing, but it's a bad strategic move for most students.

When you take an elective pass/fail, you squander the opportunity to take a course whose final grade could improve your GPA. You don't have an unlimited number of courses to take in your university career; why pass up prime opportunities to raise your GPA through great grades in well-chosen electives?

You may be concerned that if you don't seize the opportunity to learn about a new subject through an elective, you could miss out on a once-in-a-lifetime opportunity. That might have been true when your parents went to college, but don't fool yourself into believing it applies to you.

If you have your heart set on learning a particular subject, the overwhelming odds are that you can simply go online and watch—at your leisure and at no cost to you—all the lectures from a course that covers the same topic. Various websites offer thousands of classes online in numerous subjects that you can view at your convenience, and the number of courses available to watch grows exponentially every year. So don't feel obligated to use electives to enrich your education; use electives to enrich your GPA.

Online Coursework

Online coursework—courses offered partially or entirely through the internet—has become an integral part of the curriculum for many university students. Online courses vary enormously. Some are regular face-to-face courses that deliver a small portion of content online, while others offer blended instruction and deliver a large portion of content online. Still other courses take place completely online, generally with no face-to-face interaction between students and instructors.

Depending on the rules of your degree plan, you may use online courses to fulfill all types of course requirements, including general education and other introductory coursework, courses in majors and minors, and electives. Online courses may be very different from your usual face-to-face courses, but you need to treat them with the same degree of seriousness that you would every other course.

Unfortunately, too many students mistakenly assume that online courses are easy and won't require a lot of time or effort. This prompts students to make several strategic blunders. Sometimes they take online courses that they shouldn't take at all, in subjects that are ill suited for them. In other cases, students simply don't devote the time they need to excel in these courses. Occasionally they take online courses in addition to, rather than as part of, their standard load of courses, underestimating the amount of work the online courses will demand. These students quickly learn the hard way that online courses often require lots of work.

Taking courses online can be an effective way to fulfill degree requirements, but never assume that an online course will be any easier than a traditional course. Many of them actually require a greater time commitment than traditional courses. For each online course you consider, make the same kind of inquiry—if not a more thorough one—that you would for a traditional course. Only after you do some background investigation will you be able to decide whether taking a course online makes sense.

Public University Honors Programs: A Hidden Gem

These aren't a standard component of every student's degree plan, but honors programs are one of the best-kept secrets of public universities. Every year, more and more public universities offer honors programs for their top students. Many offer multiple programs. Some admit students based solely on their high school records and standardized test scores; others base admission on the GPA students earn during their first few semesters at college. Honors programs vary enormously, so you have to find out for yourself about the specifics at your university to get a sense of admission and course requirements.

Public universities often structure their honors programs to provide a small-college feel within the larger university community. They offer small discussion courses taught by great professors, extensive and personalized interaction with faculty members, academic lectures, community service projects, and a host of other enriching on- and off-campus experiences. A single university may have multiple honors programs, each with its own requirements. An honors program may be a full-fledged major plan, a multicourse sequence in your major that includes an honors thesis or senior project, a series of interdisciplinary courses in a myriad of subjects, or something else entirely.

Most honors programs provide for some sort of special honors recognition at graduation upon successful completion of the requirements. Completing an honors program can be a great way to stand out from your fellow students, making you an even stronger candidate for whatever you intend to do after you graduate, be it a job or graduate school.

You may be concerned that because the strongest students often take university honors courses, earning high grades in them may be harder than in standard courses, or that honors courses will demand more of your time. This is often a misconception. In fact, the grades in honors courses are often significantly higher than in equivalent courses that are open to all students. Professors often adjust their grading style to account for the fact that they're teaching a class composed entirely of stronger or more engaged students. Furthermore, the workloads in honors courses are often equivalent to those in regular courses. So at many universities, these concerns aren't usually valid reasons to avoid honors courses.

Regardless of whether you ultimately participate in one, be sure you spend the time to find out about the different honors programs at your university. It may turn out to be well worth your while.

PART IV

Two Key Strategies for Acing the Public University

In Part III, we explored the first GPAMaxx Cardinal Rule, Know Your University Road Map—Your Degree Plan. When you understand the requirements of your degree plan and the different ways you can fulfill them, you can position yourself to maximize your academic success.

In Part IV we explore two key alternatives—credit by examination (CBE) and transfer coursework—that you can use to fulfill significant numbers of requirements instead of taking courses at your university. When used strategically, each option can be a great way to save time and money, help ensure that you graduate on time or even early, protect your institutional GPA, and free up time for extracurricular and career-enhancing activities.

After reading Part IV, you'll be well positioned to use credit by examination and transfer coursework as strategic alternatives to satisfy your degree plan requirements while steering clear of their potential pitfalls.

CHAPTER
9

Credit by Examination: An Overview

This Chapter Covers

- Introduction to CBE
- Acceptance of CBE at public universities
- Types of exams to earn CBE

Credit by examination (CBE) refers to the practice of awarding students some form of university-level credit based solely on their satisfactory performance on an exam. The idea behind CBE is that students should get college credit for knowing a subject as well as they would if they took the equivalent university-level course. To earn CBE, students demonstrate their competency in a subject by passing an exam rather than by taking the course at their university that covers the same material. These exams are often no more than three hours long, a fraction of the time students would need to spend in the classroom and the library if they had to take the course.

Nearly all public universities award students CBE for at least some courses. Many permit students to earn CBE for up to 45 credit hours—the equivalent of three semesters' worth of courses—or more.

That's a lot of coursework that you can skip simply by passing exams instead of taking the equivalent courses. Even if your university allows you to earn only 30 credit hours toward your degree through

CBE, that's still around a full academic year's worth of course requirements you can forgo.

In cases where your university won't award credit hours based on CBE results, it may still exempt you from the equivalent course based on your exam scores. That isn't nearly as good a deal, since exemption from a course doesn't reduce the overall number of credit hours you need to graduate. At a minimum, though, it does free up space in your schedule to take other courses instead.

When universities award CBE, the vast majority do not attach a letter grade to the credit hours you earn. You get credit hours as if you'd taken the course, but no letter grade that affects your GPA. Therefore, when you earn credit hours through CBE, you only need to score high enough for your university to award you credit—and nothing more. This presents an excellent strategic opportunity, which we will discuss in more detail in the next chapter.

Types of Exams to Earn CBE

You probably know about Advanced Placement, or AP, from high school. Maybe you took or are taking some AP classes, and attempted or will attempt one or more AP exams. You might be thinking that AP is the only way to earn credit by examination, but it's not.

Many public universities allow students to earn CBE through a variety of exams. The AP exam is only one type. Take a look at your university's website or its catalog. You may be able to find out the exams for which students can earn CBE, the equivalent courses for which credit will be granted, and the minimum scores required to receive credit. In other instances, you may need to inquire with your university or the specific college or department of your major to find out all the details.

Public university students commonly earn CBE based on the results of two types of exams: those offered through national exam programs and those created by universities themselves.

National Exam Programs

In this section, we highlight four major national testing programs whose exams public universities widely accept: the Advanced Placement (AP) program, the International Baccalaureate (IB), the College-Level Examination Program (CLEP), and the DANTES Subject Standardized Tests (DSST).

A significant number of public universities will also grant students CBE based on the results of Excelsior College Examinations, SAT Subject Tests, COMPASS® exams, ACCUPLACER® exams, Cambridge International AS and A Level exams, and even various sections of the SAT and ACT. We don't discuss any of these in further detail here, but if your university offers you the opportunity to earn CBE through any of them, you should learn more about them on your own.

AP Program

The AP program, which offers high school students the opportunity to take college-level courses at their high schools, has become an increasingly common fixture in American high schools over the last few decades. Today, a majority of U.S. high schools offer their students an opportunity to take one or more AP courses.[20] In 2014, more than 2.3 million students took over 4.2 million AP exams.[21]

For many, the AP program is the gold standard of the American college preparatory curriculum. More than 90 percent of four-year colleges and universities allow students to earn credit hours, placement in more advanced coursework, or an exemption from taking a course altogether, based on achieving minimum AP exam scores.[22]

Nearly all AP courses offer students an opportunity to take a national exam, which usually includes a written component and multiple-choice questions. Students who receive a minimum satisfactory score (determined by the university they attend) can petition to receive CBE for the equivalent university course that covers the subject.

The College Board, the not-for-profit organization that administers the AP program, offered AP exams in the following subjects at press time:

- Art History
- Biology
- Calculus AB
- Calculus BC
- Chemistry
- Chinese Language and Culture
- Comparative Government and Politics
- Computer Science A
- English Language and Compositon
- English Literature and Compositon
- Environmental Science
- European History
- French Language and Culture
- German Language and Culture
- Human Geography
- Italian Language and Culture
- Japanese Language and Culture
- Latin
- Macroeconomics
- Microeconomics
- Music Theory
- Physics 1: Algebra-Based
- Physics 2: Algebra-Based
- Physics C: Electricity and Magnetism
- Physics C: Mechanics
- Psychology
- Spanish Language and Culture
- Spanish Literature and Culture
- Statistics
- United States Government and Politics
- United States History
- World History

AP exams can be a great option to earn CBE, particularly if you're taking AP classes at your high school. If you're not, you will need to plan carefully. Anyone can register to take an AP exam, but the exams are given only once a year, in the spring, and only at high schools that offer AP courses.

In contrast, the CLEP and DSST exams discussed below, among others, are offered year-round and at multiple locations in every state. If you're not enrolled in high school AP classes, taking these other exams may be a better way for you to earn CBE.

IB Program

About two percent of American high schools offer their students the opportunity to participate in the International Baccalaureate Diploma Programme, a two-year college preparatory curriculum.[23] Many universities award students CBE for college courses based on student scores on IB examinations. Unfortunately, only students enrolled in IB courses at their high schools are eligible to earn CBE through their IB coursework. If your high school doesn't participate, you're out of luck. However, if you do attend a high school with an IB program and participate in it, you'll want to find out exactly how your IB coursework can fulfill requirements at your intended university.

CLEP

The College-Level Examination Program (CLEP), which, like the AP program, is administered by the College Board, offers anyone the opportunity to take exams in a range of subjects, even if they have never taken a course that covers the tested material. You can prepare for them completely on your own. Although universities more commonly award CBE based on AP exam scores, some 2,900 institutions award CBE for one or more CLEP exams.[24] Further, most public universities award CBE for at least some CLEP exams.

The College Board offered CLEP exams in the following subjects at press time:

Business

- Financial Accounting
- Information Systems and Computer Applications
- Introductory Business Law
- Principles of Management
- Principles of Marketing

Composition and Literature

- American Literature
- Analyzing and Interpreting Literature
- College Composition
- College Composition Modular
- English Literature
- Humanities

History and Social Sciences

- American Government
- History of the United States I: Early Colonization to 1877
- History of the United States II: 1865 to the Present
- Human Growth and Development
- Introduction to Educational Psychology
- Introductory Psychology
- Introductory Sociology
- Principles of Macroeconomics
- Principles of Microeconomics
- Social Sciences and History
- Western Civilization I: Ancient Near East to 1648
- Western Civilization II: 1648 to the Present

Science and Mathematics

- Biology
- Calculus
- Chemistry
- College Algebra
- College Mathematics
- Natural Sciences
- Precalculus

World Languages

- French Language (Levels 1 and 2)
- German Language (Levels 1 and 2)
- Spanish Language (Levels 1 and 2)

CLEP exams offer several significant advantages over AP exams.

From a convenience standpoint, CLEP exams involve far fewer logistical hurdles. You may take the exams at any time throughout the year, allowing you to prepare on your own schedule. Every state has multiple CLEP testing centers, and you can sometimes even take them on a walk-in basis. That flexibility can be a game changer.

Another advantage lies in the format of CLEP exams. Most consist solely of multiple-choice questions that you take by computer, with scores available immediately after you complete the exam. This allows you to learn quickly whether your score on a CLEP exam qualifies for CBE at your university. With this information in mind, you can then plan your upcoming course schedule with certainty and better develop your overall college game plan.

A further advantage of CLEP exams is that the College Board allows students to repeat each exam every six months. If you don't score high enough to earn CBE for a subject the first time you take the applicable CLEP exam, you can take it again six months later.

Another plus: CLEP exams cover many of the same subjects as AP and IB exams. So even if you're planning to take an AP or IB exam, you should always take the corresponding CLEP exam as well if your intended university awards CBE for that exam. Be sure to take the CLEP test while the material is still fresh in your mind. You'll have your CLEP results long before you receive your AP or IB exam scores.

DSST Program

The DSST program, also known as DANTES, offers students the opportunity to take more than 30 exams. Over 2,000 institutions award CBE based on DSST exam results.[25] The exams primarily cover subjects that meet general education and other introductory requirements.

Like most CLEP exams, DSST exams are in a multiple-choice format, and nearly all can be scored immediately after you complete the exam. You learn right away whether you scored high enough to earn CBE for a course. This allows you to make your academic planning decisions in real time rather than having to wait for your exam results.

DSST exams are offered in the following subjects at press time:

Business

- Business Ethics and Society
- Business Mathematics
- Human Resource Management
- Introduction to Business
- Introduction to Computing
- Management Information Systems

- Organizational Behavior
- Personal Finance

- Principles of Finance
- Principles of Supervision

Humanities

- Ethics in America
- Introduction to World Religions

- Principles of Public Speaking

Mathematics

- Fundamentals of College Algebra

- Principles of Statistics

Physical Science

- Astronomy
- Environment and Humanity: The Race to Save the Planet

- Here's to Your Health
- Principles of Physical Science I

Social Sciences

- A History of the Vietnam War
- Art of the Western World
- Criminal Justice
- Foundations of Education
- Fundamentals of Counseling
- Human/Cultural Geography

- Introduction to Law Enforcement
- Lifespan Developmental Psychology
- Substance Abuse
- The Civil War and Reconstruction

Technology

- Fundamentals of Cybersecurity
- Technical Writing

University-Specific Exams

Many universities design their own exams through which students can earn CBE. The exams, as well as their structure and content, vary greatly depending on the university and even on the faculty members who create them.

Some universities combine an exam offered by one of the national testing services with an essay or other written portion prepared by faculty members. Universities use these hybridized exams when they want to ensure that the knowledge the exam tests is functionally equivalent to the material taught in the course on campus.

Students who want to take these exams should inquire with their university. Often, when students attend freshman orientation, their university requires them to take one or more of these exams— commonly in English, math, and any foreign language they may have studied in high school—to ensure placement in appropriate-level courses. At many public universities, students can earn credit hours and fulfill degree plan requirements based on the results of these exams. Less often, students receive exemptions from an equivalent course or are placed into a higher-level course, but don't receive credit hours based on their performance.

Keep in mind that your university may provide you with other opportunities to earn CBE, even in subjects that don't have a standard exam to demonstrate your knowledge. For example, if you speak a language not tested by one of the standard exams, are a foreign student with advanced levels of education that aren't easily transferable to an American university, or have otherwise acquired specialized academic knowledge, your university may allow you to earn CBE for equivalent courses in those subjects. If you fit this description, it's even more essential that you familiarize yourself with your university's CBE policies so you can get college credit for what you already know.

National Exams for International Students

If you completed high school or its equivalent outside the United States, you may have an opportunity to earn credit hours toward your degree that is unavailable to American students. A number of universities award as many as 30 credit hours (a typical year's worth of university coursework) to students who have successfully passed national exams like the German *Abitur*, the A-Levels in the United Kingdom and their equivalent in many British Commonwealth countries, the French *Baccalauréate*, and the Italian *Maturita*. A student who has passed the German *Abitur* or the Italian *Maturita*, for example, may be eligible to begin college in the United States as a sophomore, receiving credit hours for coursework in subjects she has already been tested on in her country's national exam.

Universities don't always publicize the options available for their foreign students to obtain credit hours for prior learning. This shouldn't come as a surprise. After all, most of you pay much higher tuition than state residents and are often ineligible for financial aid. Your university would probably prefer that you spend a full four years—or even longer—filling its coffers as a full-tuition-paying student. Therefore, you need to inquire with your university as to your options.

If your university won't award you credit hours based on your country's national exam, you can still leverage your knowledge by taking exams to earn as much CBE as possible. Because of the often much more rigorous academic standards in other countries' equivalents to high school, you may be well prepared to test out of many of your general education and other introductory courses through CBE.

In any case, you must be proactive and make an effort to find out all your options to earn college credit for what you already know. If you don't learn about the options you have, then you won't have any.

Making the Most of Credit by Examination

This Chapter Covers

- Strategic advantages of CBE
- Pitfalls of CBE
- Preparing for exams to earn CBE
- Prioritizing your use of CBE

The previous chapter provided a basic introduction to credit by examination. This chapter examines CBE in greater depth. First, we discuss the significant strategic advantages that you can derive by using CBE. We also point out some of the pitfalls you need to avoid when you develop your personalized CBE strategy. Then we tell you how you can prepare independently to earn CBE, and suggest how you should prioritize the order in which you prepare for exams on your own.

Strategic Advantages to Using Credit by Examination

Using credit by examination to fulfill course requirements under your degree plan can be a great strategic tool. Studies have shown that students who earn CBE and skip an entry-level college course typically perform better in higher-level courses in the same subject than their classmates.[26] Studies have also found that students who earn CBE generally have higher college GPAs than those who don't.[27] These are valid reasons for you to utilize CBE, but there are a number of other practical and strategic advantages as well. Here are some of the ways that CBE can potentially help you.

Save Significant Amounts of Money

Some public universities charge for tuition by the credit hour. If you attend one of them, any credit hour you complete through CBE saves you money. The fewer credit hours you take, the fewer you pay for.

And that's not the only way CBE can save you money. If the credit hours you earn through CBE enable you to graduate early, you can enjoy huge potential cost savings and other financial benefits. As we discussed in Chapter 1, when you add up tuition and fees, room and board, and other college-related and personal expenses, the average cost of a year at a public university for an in-state student exceeds $23,400. If you can graduate a semester or a year early, that's many thousands of dollars that you or your parents won't have to shell out.

That's not even the biggest financial benefit for you, though. By shortening your time as a college student, you can potentially enter the workforce sooner and start making money instead of just spending it. Using CBE to eliminate even one semester from your college education can mean thousands of dollars in savings and significantly more in earnings. Any way you look at it, these combined amounts can be a lot of money.

Graduate Early

If you earn credit hours through CBE for a significant number of required college courses, you may be able to complete your degree ahead of schedule and graduate early. Every year, increasing numbers of students graduate early thanks to the credit hours they earned through CBE. However, graduating early requires meticulous planning. If you think you may want to graduate early, it's especially critical that you begin developing a game plan to complete your degree requirements before you even start college. In Chapter 16, we'll show you how to develop your own step-by-step university game plan. Once you work your way through those steps, you can start moving toward that goal.

Ensure Graduation in Four Years

Even if CBE doesn't put you in a position to graduate from college early, it can help ensure that you graduate on time. Every course you fulfill through CBE is a course you don't have to take. That makes CBE an outstanding way to get a jump on the course requirements you need to complete your degree. The unfortunate reality is that less than a third of today's public university students graduate within four years, and barely half graduate within five. CBE can help ensure that you graduate on time.

Take a Lighter Course Load

Not everyone wants to graduate early. CBE can give you a head start on coursework, which in turn may allow you to take a lighter course load during one or more semesters. This can leave you with more time to focus on the courses you do take.

A lighter course load also opens room in your schedule to enrich your college experience outside of the classroom. You might, for example, get more involved in on-campus extracurricular activities or enjoy a more active social life than you would have with a heavier course load. As we discussed in Chapter 4, such activities aren't just fun. They can also be great ways to expand your skill set and build a strong network of professional and social contacts.

Steer Clear of Difficult Required Courses That Can Hurt Your GPA

As we discussed in Chapter 9, students most often use credit by examination to fulfill general education and other introductory-level course requirements. Those courses can pose a great threat to your GPA because earning a good grade in them is often so difficult. Maybe you're weak or completely uninterested in the subject. Or perhaps the professor grades the course on a harsh curve. Whatever the reason, you should try to avoid taking courses that put your GPA at high risk.

CBE can help you deal with those types of courses. If you're successful and earn CBE for them, you don't have to take the courses at all. That eliminates their potential to hurt your GPA.

By now, you're probably asking yourself: if a course would be tough for you at your university, how can you possibly hope to score high enough on an exam to earn CBE for it? It's a good question, and the answer isn't obvious.

Most students are stuck in the mindset that they need the highest grade they can get on an exam to earn CBE, just as they would want if they were taking the course. As a result, they often don't even bother trying to earn CBE in subjects in which they have a decent chance of passing but not acing their exams. Generally, this is the wrong way to approach CBE.

You need to think of CBE as something completely different from the courses themselves. In most cases, to earn CBE for a course, you only need to pass the exam with the lowest score your university will accept. At many public universities, the lowest passing score is equivalent to a C grade. On CLEP exams, for example, students often qualify for CBE when they earn a scaled score of at least 50 out of 80 points. Thus, to earn CBE for a course, you only need to know the subject matter well enough to scrape by.

Further, as we discussed earlier, you usually don't receive a letter grade for your score. Your university transcript likely indicates only that you earned CBE and credit hours for the course. No one will ever know how well you did on the exam, even if you barely passed. Plus there's no harm in trying. Even if you don't pass, the fact that you attempted the exam won't appear on your university transcript.

These exams are actually more like pass/fail courses than your regular graded ones. You earn credit hours and fulfill requirements toward your degree, but without any negative impact on your GPA. Especially in your weaker subject areas, this can be an effective way to fulfill degree requirements without putting your GPA at risk.

Gain Priority for Course Registration

By earning a sufficient number of credit hours through CBE, you may be able to register for your courses before your classmates who began college with you.

Many public universities classify students as freshmen, sophomores, juniors, or seniors based not on how long they've been on campus, but on the number of credit hours they've earned. For example, you may be in only your second semester and think of yourself as a freshman, but because you arrived at college with CBE for more than a semester's worth of credit hours, your university classifies you as a sophomore rather than as a freshman. This can have big advantages, particularly when it comes to registering for courses.

Public universities usually use a priority system to determine the order in which students register for classes. Generally, seniors have priority to register before juniors, juniors before sophomores, and sophomores before freshmen. So even if you're in your second semester of college, if you earned CBE for a semester's worth of credit hours, you get to register for your courses with the sophomores—before the freshmen who started with you.

The earlier you get to register for your courses, the better your chances of getting a spot in the courses you want, with the professors you want. At many universities, each semester's course registration period brings about a stampede—usually an online one—as students race to register for the most popular courses, discussion sections, and instructors. Students with lower priority often don't get their first or even second choices. They can easily get stuck with "leftover" courses and instructors that nobody else wants.

When courses are filled, sometimes students can't enroll in courses they need to graduate. As a result, they fall behind on required coursework and have to delay graduation. You can more easily avoid these types of situations when the credit hours you've earned through CBE give you priority to register ahead of the other students from your year.

Focus on the Courses That Are Most Important to Your Future

Many students spend their first year of college primarily taking courses that fulfill general education requirements rather than courses that interest them or are more relevant to their academic and career goals. By earning CBE, you can focus sooner and more extensively on the classes that really matter to you and your plans.

Obviously, this allows you to focus on your major at an earlier stage of your college career. But there's a much bigger advantage than just that: with space in your course schedule freed up, you can take additional courses to develop specific skills and gain knowledge that makes you a more attractive candidate to future employers and graduate schools. This might mean that you pick up a second major, write a senior thesis, study abroad, learn a foreign language more intensively, or take specific courses with an eye toward increasing your appeal to employers. In each case, CBE can help you gain time to focus on coursework that's a priority for you.

Learning by Example

To show you how you can use CBE to your advantage, here's the story of one rising public university student who benefited from earning credit hours through CBE.

Megan, a recent high school graduate, will attend State University as an International Business major beginning this fall. After college, she wants to pursue a career in international business with a focus on Asia. Megan hopes to study abroad in China and become fluent in Chinese, a language she's never studied, before she graduates from State University. Achieving these goals will be tough.

Because she knew she'd have a lot to accomplish at State University, Megan got a jump on her college requirements while still in high school. Before her junior year, she found out which exams could earn her CBE for specific degree requirements at State University. She then enrolled in several AP classes whose exams could potentially earn her CBE. Megan's high school counselor suggested she also take AP Human Geography and AP Environmental Science, but she rejected that advice because State University wouldn't award CBE for passing either of those exams.

When Megan found out which exams could earn her CBE at State University, she learned that State University would also award CBE for several CLEP and DSST exams that covered the same subjects as some of her high school classes. She made time in her busy schedule to study for a number of those exams, too.

Before she graduated from high school, Megan took the following 11 exams:

- AP Biology
- AP Chemistry
- AP Art History
- AP U.S. Government and Politics
- CLEP Introductory Psychology
- CLEP English Literature
- CLEP History of the United States I
- CLEP History of the United States II
- CLEP Calculus
- CLEP American Government
- DSST Art of the Western World

Much to her surprise, Megan managed to score high enough on all but three exams to earn CBE at State University. She took the AP U.S. Government and Politics exam as well as the corresponding CLEP American Government exam, but unfortunately didn't earn a passing score on either. Megan also didn't score sufficiently high on the AP Art History exam, but she earned CBE for the equivalent course at State University by passing the DSST Art of the Western World exam, which covers similar material.

Although Megan earned CBE for the other eight exams, she didn't exactly ace them all. In fact, on some of them, her score barely qualified for CBE. A couple of the exams were in subjects—American history and English literature—that gave Megan considerable trouble in high school. But by using good review materials that taught to the exams and built on what she had learned in her high school classes in the same subjects, she scored high enough to get college credit. The fact that Megan merely scraped by on several of the exams is now irrelevant. State University awards only credit hours and not letter grades for passing scores, so she only needed the lowest score acceptable to State University.

State University awards CBE for the one-semester course equivalents of each of the six CLEP and DSST exams Megan passed. Each course is three credit hours. That adds up to a total of 18 credit hours she won't have to take.

Even better, for the AP Biology and AP Chemistry exams she passed, State University awards course credit for two semesters of introductory biology and introductory chemistry. Each semester is four credit hours. That's an additional 16 credit hours she won't have to worry about.

All in all, Megan will receive CBE for 10 courses, or a total of 34 credit hours toward her degree, which requires 120 credit hours to graduate. Although she hasn't even started at State University, Megan has already earned credit hours equivalent to more than two semesters of coursework, or over 25 percent of the total she'll need to graduate. Essentially, she'll start college as a sophomore rather than a freshman.

Megan's success was due to more than just taking a lot of exams. Choosing her exams strategically played a huge role. Let's take a closer look at the distribution requirements of Megan's degree plan and how many of them she has already fulfilled with CBE.

General Education Distribution	Degree Requirement	Megan's Progress
Natural sciences	4 courses	Her passing scores on the AP Biology and AP Chemistry exams satisfy the entire requirement. She doesn't need to take any natural sciences courses.
Social sciences	1 course	Her passing score on the CLEP Introductory Psychology exam satisfies the entire requirement.
English language	2 courses	By passing the CLEP English Literature exam, she earned CBE for one of the two English language course requirements. She must take one more course in this distribution.
American history	2 courses	Her passing scores on the two CLEP American history exams satisfy the entire requirement. She doesn't need to take any American history courses.
Mathematics	2 courses	By passing the CLEP Calculus exam, she earned CBE for one of the two mathematics course requirements. She must take one more course in this distribution.
Fine arts	1 course	Her passing score on the DSST Art of the Western World exam satisfies the entire requirement. She doesn't need to take any fine arts courses.

By satisfying so many degree plan requirements through CBE before she even begins college, Megan has opened a world of opportunities for herself. Depending on the specific decisions she makes, she can:

- **Graduate early and save a lot of money.** Because Megan earned CBE for more than a year's worth of her required coursework, she may be well positioned to finish her undergraduate degree early, saving both time and money. Unlike many students who want to graduate early, Megan won't necessarily have to take extra courses each semester— which could risk leaving her overwhelmed and limit her involvement in extracurricular and social activities. She may even want to take additional exams to earn CBE in other subjects that further position her to graduate early (for example, in the foreign language she took in high school).

- **Ensure she's able to graduate on time in four years.** Even if Megan doesn't want to graduate early, by earning CBE for more than a year's worth of college credit, Megan has built 34 credit hours of flexibility into her course schedule. That will give her more flexibility to take all the other courses she needs to graduate on time.

- **Take a lighter course load each semester.** Because she's already earned CBE for 10 courses, she may be able to take a lighter course load each semester (if she doesn't want to graduate early). A typical student at State University must complete an average of 15 credit hours per semester to complete 120 credit hours over four years. But because Megan has already earned 34 credit hours through CBE, she may only have to enroll in around 12 credit hours per semester. This would allow her to devote more time to the courses she does take.

  A lighter course load may also give Megan more time to participate in social and extracurricular activities. She might pledge a sorority, get involved in activities related to her major and interest in Asia, or do something else—in addition to the activities she could have comfortably managed with a heavier course load. Extracurricular and social activities aren't just enjoyable; well-chosen ones can greatly broaden her skill set and her potential network of contacts, which can provide an edge when Megan applies for internships and jobs.

- **Complete degree requirements without affecting her GPA.** General education courses can be some of the riskiest ones for public university students and their GPAs. By earning CBE for 10 of her general education courses, Megan eliminated the risk that those course grades could have posed to her GPA had she taken the courses at State University. Megan barely scraped by on a number of the exams, and she earned CBE for two courses in subjects that gave her trouble in high school. It therefore seems unlikely she would have done well in all of those courses at State University. But by earning CBE for 10 courses, she has managed to do an end run around several potential threats to her GPA.

- **Have priority for course registration over the other students who started with her.** Because Megan will arrive at State University with more than an entire year's worth of credit hours, the university will likely classify her as a sophomore for her second semester. That means she'll be able to register for her second-semester courses as a sophomore, before her classmates who remain classified as freshmen. This may enable Megan to register for more of her first-choice courses and professors, rather than potentially having to settle for the undesirable ones that await her classmates who have lower priority because they are still considered freshmen.

- **Focus on courses that will benefit her plans.** Because Megan has managed to fulfill so many of her general education course requirements through CBE, she can focus her studies on courses in her major and other subject areas that interest her. Since Megan hopes to work in Asia after graduation, she can pursue that goal from the day she starts at State University. For example, she can take courses in her International Business major sooner and develop greater expertise in that field. She may now also have room in her schedule to take more courses in Chinese, and may be able to study abroad in China for a couple of semesters. She might even want to add a second major, in Asian Studies or Chinese. These types of measures can make her a more desirable candidate when she applies for internships and jobs.

A Pitfall of Credit by Examination: Accepting Credit for an Introductory Class, Then Struggling in the Follow-Up Course

There are many good reasons to use CBE to maximize your success at college, but it isn't always the best strategic option.

Although students who earn CBE often do well in advanced courses in the same subject, they run the risk that CBE will leave them without the foundation they need to succeed in higher-level courses. This danger is particularly acute in subjects that require both an introductory course and a follow-up course (or courses). If you think you'll have trouble with the follow-up course, you should carefully consider whether bypassing that all-important first course makes sense for you.

Always weigh the potential variables before you decide to accept CBE for a course, even if your score qualifies. Just because you can doesn't mean you always should.

Learning by Example

Let's look at an example of a student who will want to consider carefully whether CBE makes sense for him.

Craig, a recent high school graduate, is about to begin his first semester at State University. He plans to major in statistics. In an attempt to earn CBE for Introduction to Statistics at State University, he took both the AP Statistics and the DSST Principles of Statistics exams. His score on the AP exam didn't qualify him for CBE, but his DSST score did—just barely. He earned the lowest possible passing score. Craig must now decide whether to accept CBE or take the State University course.

For many students, accepting CBE for the DSST exam would be a smart strategic move—if it merely fulfilled a general education course requirement. However, Craig plans to major in statistics. Introduction to Statistics serves as the foundation for all subsequent statistics courses required of statistics majors, so Craig really needs a solid grasp of statistics fundamentals. To give himself the best chance at success in subsequent statistics courses, he may be better off taking the actual course, despite his passing DSST exam score.

Ultimately, Craig's decision may rest on whether he can gain a solid grasp of the fundamental concepts taught in Introduction to Statistics without taking the actual course. Today, students have a number of ways to do this. Craig might, for example, simply review books, video lectures, and other online materials relating to statistics. Since every student's situation is different, before he reaches a decision, Craig will want to evaluate the options he has to gain the solid foundation he will need for future statistics courses.

Learning by Example

Because it's important to think strategically when deciding whether to accept the credit hours that you earn through CBE and the resulting placement in a higher-level course, let's look at another example that illustrates how CBE can leave you in over your head.

Jackie, a recent high school graduate, will be a freshman at State University this fall. Jackie took four years of high school Spanish. At the end of her senior year of high school, she took the CLEP Spanish Language Level 2 exam and scored high enough to earn CBE for three semesters of introductory Spanish at State University. However, the foreign language distribution of her degree plan requires her to complete four sequential semesters of introductory Spanish.

If Jackie petitions State University to receive CBE for all three courses, she'll begin her Spanish studies in the fourth-semester course of the introductory sequence, which may be quite challenging for her. Jackie has to decide whether to petition for CBE for all three semesters for which she's eligible.

College foreign language courses can be very different from those in high school. Even though she earned CBE for three semesters of college Spanish, Jackie's language proficiency may not neatly align with what she's expected to know for fourth-semester college Spanish. This puts her at risk of entering fourth-semester Spanish insufficiently prepared, which could result in a low grade that could hurt her GPA.

As a result, Jackie may prefer to petition for CBE for only the initial two semesters of Spanish. By beginning her language sequence with the third-semester college Spanish course, she can help ensure that she has the foundation she needs to thrive in her State University Spanish courses.

Regardless of how she proceeds, Jackie must think strategically. Making the wrong decision could have serious negative consequences for her GPA.

Earning CBE vs. Going for the A in the College Course

Most public universities don't record a letter grade for credit hours earned through CBE. You get credit for the course, but no letter grade that gets averaged into your GPA. If you're like many students, you may think that earning CBE for courses in your best subjects means giving up an opportunity to earn easy As by taking the college courses that cover the same topics. Before you decide to forgo CBE and take a particular course on campus instead, though, keep a few things in mind.

For starters, you shouldn't ever assume that any university course will be an easy A, especially when it comes to general education and other introductory courses. As we discussed in Chapter 8, these courses can prove to be much more difficult than their high school equivalents. So even if you aced your AP Chemistry exam in high school, there's no guarantee that you'll repeat your performance in the introductory chemistry course at your university. You're not the only student who excelled in high school chemistry. If you take the course, you may face stiff competition to get an A from other students who also aced high school chemistry.

Also remember that earning CBE for a course frees up room in your schedule for a different course. You might, for instance, accept CBE for one course and then take a different course that provides additional credit hours toward your degree but covers a lot of the same material. For example, if you earn CBE for the CLEP History of the United States I exam, which covers American history through 1877, you could take a course on campus that covers Colonial American history. With your strong background in early American history, you might be positioned to excel in that one as well. And best of all, it would earn you additional credit hours toward your degree.

Whenever you face these decisions, always think strategically and weigh your options. Unless there's a compelling reason not to take advantage of CBE, it may be best to accept CBE even in your stronger subjects.

Preparing on Your Own for Exams to Earn Credit by Examination

Unfortunately, while large numbers of students earn some CBE for college courses, only a very small percentage ever take full advantage of all the opportunities they have to earn CBE and maximize the credit hours that they earn through it. Too many high school and college students mistakenly believe that they have to take a formal class that directly prepares them for an exam. It never occurs to them that they could prepare on their own.

As a result, many students take the exams offered in connection with their AP and IB classes in high school, and the mandatory placement exams at their university's freshman orientation in core subjects like English and math, but that's it. They never explore further options to earn CBE. Even after they start college, students remain trapped in the mindset that they can't earn CBE by studying for exams without taking a formal class. They spend an entire semester taking courses on campus for which they would have had a good chance of earning CBE, if only they had they spent a few weeks studying on their own to pass the exams.

This is a real missed opportunity. Many of you don't need to take any type of organized class that prepares you for an exam to earn CBE. If you are motivated and willing to put in the hours, you can prepare for any number of exams on your own. There are plenty of resources that can help you prepare independently for exams that can earn you CBE. It's up to you, however, to take the first step and get started with your review.

The following are a couple of ways that you can prepare for exams to earn CBE on your own.

Using Study Guides and Online Review Materials

Exam preparation is big business. Multiple publishers offer review books for the more popular exams that qualify students to earn CBE. These guides, which contain detailed summaries and explanations of the subject matter as well as practice exams, may teach you all you need to earn CBE for any number of courses. These guides may be at your local public library, or you can buy them online or at a local bookstore. The $20 or $30 you spend for each book is a whole lot less than the tuition for the equivalent course at your university.

If you learn more effectively online, you're also in luck. A growing number of companies offer students online review materials and practice exams to prepare for specific exams. You can find them with a simple web search. Some of these companies offer free exam preparation online, while others charge a fee to access their review materials.

Preparing Through Free Online Courses

Many students don't like to learn strictly on their own without the benefit of an instructor who can explain complicated concepts. Thankfully, when it comes to preparing for exams to earn CBE, they no longer have to.

Today, a growing number of free online courses prepare students specifically for exams that can earn them CBE. The Saylor Foundation (www.saylor.org), for example, offers free online courses you can take to prepare for multiple CLEP and other exams at your own pace.

On the websites for Academic Earth (www.academicearth.org) and the Open Education Consortium (www.oeconsortium.org), for example, you can access online for free the lectures and materials of many previously recorded university-level courses in their entirety. These include some of the general education courses for which you can take exams to earn CBE. Think of these online courses as a tuition-free education—or a tuition-free way to earn CBE. Generally, you watch a semester's worth of lectures in a particular course, download and regularly review the accompanying course materials, and then take a final exam. In your case, your final exam will be a CLEP, DSST, or other exam to earn CBE.

If you are less of an independent learner and more the type who prefers to interact with other students in an actual college-level course, a new but expanding online option exists: massive open online courses, or **MOOCs**. MOOCs are university-level online courses that are open to anyone who wishes to register for them, listen to the course lectures, and participate over the internet. Two of the best-known providers of MOOCs are Coursera (www.coursera.com) and edX (www.edX.org). At press time, both allow anyone to register at no charge for the online courses they offer.

Because most universities don't currently award credit hours for successfully completing a MOOC, simply enrolling in one isn't enough. You need to find a way to transform what you learn through your participation in a MOOC into credit hours toward your degree. CBE provides you a way to do this. If your university awards CBE for a course that covers the same content as the MOOC, you can earn CBE for the course by taking the relevant CLEP or other exam to demonstrate what you learned in the MOOC.

To improve your odds of earning CBE through a free online course, you will probably still want to supplement your online learning with some serious reading from one of the review books for the specific exam you will take. This can sharply increase your odds of scoring high enough on an exam to earn CBE.

Prioritizing Your Use of Credit by Examination

To maximize your use of CBE, you need to decide which exams to attempt as well as the order in which to take them. This will require you to make some choices. After all, you likely won't have the time to prepare for exams in every subject for which you can earn college credit. Therefore, you need to prioritize.

Why Sooner Is Usually Better

For nearly all students, it makes sense to begin taking exams to earn CBE as early as possible. That means before you start college, ideally while you're still in high school. There are usually no advantages to waiting. In any event, try to pass as many exams as you can before you even begin at your university. Take advantage of any time you have now to do this. Once you start college, you're going to have your hands full with your regular classes. Freeing up time in your schedule then to prepare on your own to earn CBE may be more difficult than you think.

There are other strategic reasons why earning CBE sooner rather than later is preferable. Some public universities allow students to earn CBE only before they complete their first semester. Even if you attend a university that allows you to earn CBE at any time before you graduate, try to fulfill requirements through CBE as soon as you can. If you wait to take exams to earn CBE until late in your undergraduate career, you put yourself at risk of lacking courses you need to graduate.

Order of Taking Exams to Earn CBE

In Chapter 16, you will learn a step-by-step approach to develop your own university game plan. As part of this game plan, you will create an action plan to incorporate CBE into your degree completion strategy and prioritize the order in which you plan to attempt exams. Different students will want to take different exams in varying orders, depending on their own situations.

The extent to which you can use CBE to fulfill degree plan requirements and the action plan you develop depends on several factors: your university's policies, where you are in your studies, the strength of your academic preparedness for college-level work, and your time and motivation to prepare for exams. The order for taking exams suggested here is geared especially to those of you who fit the following profile:

- You want to be a strong student who maximizes your use of CBE and your college GPA

- You have yet to begin your freshman year at college

- You want to graduate from college on time, or maybe even early

- You are motivated to invest the time and effort needed to prepare for exams

For those of you who don't match this profile, the number of exams you take, and the order in which you take them, may differ. But if you fit the profile above, consider prioritizing your CBE action plan in the following order:

1. **If you're currently in high school and taking AP or IB courses, focus foremost on scoring sufficiently high on those exams to earn CBE.**

   If the university you will attend awards CBE for AP and/or IB exam scores, focus on the exams for the AP and/or IB courses you take in high school. Those exams can be very challenging, so make sure you adequately prepare for them. Even if you feel you have an excellent grasp of these subjects, don't ever assume you'll score high enough to earn CBE. Study more than you feel is necessary.

Take Out an Insurance Policy: Attempt Multiple Exams to Earn CBE in the Same Subject

If you're a high school student who will take AP or IB exams, keep in mind that your intended university may also award CBE based on the results of other exams that test the same subjects. For example, your intended university may award CBE based not only on the results of the AP Biology and Chemistry exams, but on the CLEP Biology and Chemistry exams as well. Any time your intended university awards CBE for passing the CLEP or a different exam in the same subject as one of your AP or IB exams, take that other exam as an insurance policy.

By taking more than one exam to earn CBE in a subject, you double your chances to earn CBE. And if it later turns out that you didn't score high enough on the AP or IB exam to earn CBE, you might have succeeded on the other exam.

Before you take any AP or IB exam, or as soon as possible afterward, take the CLEP or other exam as well. Don't wait! You want to take the exam while the material you learned preparing for the AP or IB exam is fresh in your mind. You won't find out your AP and IB exam scores for more than a month. If you wait to take an alternate exam until you receive your AP or IB exam results, you'll likely forget much of what you learned.

2. **Take exams that fulfill general education and other introductory requirements in your weakest subjects.**

Focus on your weakest subjects? Isn't that backward? Shouldn't you only take exams in subjects for which you have an excellent chance to earn CBE?

Absolutely not. Remember that to earn CBE, you don't have to ace the exam. You only have to earn the minimum score required by your university—and nothing more. When students earn CBE for a course, most universities award only credit hours—without a letter grade. If you can squeak by with a passing score, you do an end run around the course completely, without receiving a grade that could lower your GPA. In your weakest subjects, this is no small feat.

Another reason to take exams to earn CBE in your weakest subjects as soon as possible is to preserve your options. If you don't score high enough to earn CBE, you still want to avoid taking what will likely be a difficult course at your university. You'll want to consider other options, such as taking the exam a second time, or taking an alternate exam that fulfills the same requirement for your degree. If none of those approaches works, you might be able to fulfill the requirement by taking the course for transfer credit at a different college.

Time can be your biggest enemy. If you don't prioritize and fulfill requirements in your weaker subjects through CBE, you may have little choice other than to take those courses at your university. Whenever possible, this is something you want to avoid.

3. **Take exams to earn CBE for courses you must complete during your first year of college.**

Many universities require their students to complete certain general education and introductory requirements during their freshman year. If you do not attempt to earn CBE for each, you forfeit the opportunity when you take the course freshman year.

Once you take exams to earn CBE in your weakest subjects, prepare for exams to earn CBE in mandatory freshman courses. Even if you don't feel adequately prepared for a particular exam, you should still take it. If you score high enough to earn CBE, you will be very glad you did.

4. **Take exams in subjects that you took in high school or for which you otherwise possess knowledge or skill—as long as the exams satisfy course requirements toward your degree.**

Since you already have prior knowledge in these areas, you may be able to earn CBE without investing very much time preparing for the exams. Don't forget that you won't need to demonstrate complete mastery of the material on these exams; you only have to pass with the lowest score your university will accept.

You want to take these exams sooner rather than later. The longer you wait, the less likely it becomes that you will fully remember all that you've learned. Leverage what you already know.

5. Take exams to satisfy any remaining nonelective degree requirements.

If you have time for additional exams, focus on the ones for any remaining required general education and introductory courses. These may even be in subjects with which you aren't very familiar because you've never studied them. You can prepare for these exams on your own using various types of review materials, some of which we discuss earlier in this chapter. With adequate preparation, many motivated students earn CBE in subjects that were previously unfamiliar to them. Perhaps you can as well.

6. Take exams to fulfill elective course requirements.

Generally speaking, using CBE to satisfy elective course requirements should be your lowest priority. Wisely chosen elective courses, after all, offer you a great opportunity to boost your GPA, something CBE does not. Nevertheless, given all the strategic advantages of CBE over taking actual courses, it can still make sense to use CBE to fulfill elective course requirements, especially if you want to graduate early. So if you have the time, prepare for exams in subjects for which you can earn CBE in elective courses.

When you develop an action plan to use CBE as part of your college completion game plan after you read Chapter 16, you will want to refer to this information to help you.

Taking Transfer Courses: An Overview

This Chapter Covers

- Introduction to transfer courses
- Dual enrollment
- Strategic advantages of taking transfer courses
- Potential pitfalls of transfer courses

If you currently or will attend a public university, it's unlikely that you're required to complete all of your coursework there. Rather, you're usually permitted to take a significant number of courses at other colleges. If your university recognizes a course at another college as equivalent to one of its own courses, it will often award you credit hours toward your degree if you take it at the other college. These courses are often called **transfer courses** because students transfer the credit for them from the college where they take them to the university where they pursue their degree.

Transfer Courses vs. Courses at Your University

Depending on the university you attend, you may be able to use transfer courses to satisfy all types of course requirements, ranging from general education courses to specialized ones in your major. However, there are two critical differences between transfer courses and those you take at your university.

First, a majority of public universities don't include the grades from most transfer courses in the institutional GPA. Students at those universities receive credit hours for transfer courses and fulfill degree requirements, but the grades they earn in those courses don't count in the calculation of their institutional GPA. Rather, those grades affect only their cumulative GPA.

Second, many states require their public universities to award credit hours for transfer courses taken at other public colleges in the same state. It doesn't matter if you take a course for transfer credit at the leading state university or at a local community college, or if the college has a good or bad reputation academically. Under state law, your university may have no choice but to award you credit hours toward your degree for equivalent courses.

These differences can have big implications for you. For example, if you successfully complete multiple general education courses at a community college during your summer break, your university may be required to award you credit hours toward your degree for the equivalent courses—but without grades that affect your institutional GPA. Using transfer courses to fulfill degree plan requirements strategically can really benefit you academically and help you maintain your institutional GPA.

Taking Transfer Courses in the Same State Is Usually Straightforward

Determining whether you can receive credit hours for transfer courses is often easy. Contracts between schools known as **articulation agreements** require many public universities to recognize and award transfer credit for equivalent courses taken at other public colleges in the same state, including community colleges. These agreements articulate exactly which courses are equivalent to one another.

A growing number of states also require their public colleges to use a common numbering system for undergraduate courses. Where this exists, equivalent courses at all public colleges in that state have the same course number. If the state in which you study has a common course numbering system, it's usually easy and straightforward to identify courses you can take at other in-state public colleges to earn credit hours toward your degree.

Just to be on the safe side, however, always confirm with your university that every class you want to take for transfer credit will fulfill an equivalent course requirement at your university, and that the credit hours transfer. You never want to take a course at another college, only to find out later that your own university won't accept the credit hours.

College Courses in High School: Dual Enrollment

Taking AP and IB courses isn't the only way high school students can earn college-level credit for work they complete in high school. Many high school students can earn high school and college credit simultaneously through an arrangement known by a variety of names, including dual enrollment, dual credit, and concurrent enrollment.

The structure of **dual enrollment** courses varies widely, but it commonly looks like this: high school students enroll in a course sponsored by a local two- or four-year college, often held at their own high school and taught by a high school teacher with some additional training. The course covers the material taught in the regular high school course as well as the corresponding college-level course at the local college. Upon successfully completing the dual enrollment course, students receive credit from their high school and college credit hours from the college that sponsored it. Dual enrollment thereby provides students with an introduction to college-level coursework as well as an opportunity to earn college-level credit while they are still in high school.

Dual enrollment programs have proliferated in recent years and are more widespread than ever. In fact, more than three-quarters of all U.S. high schools offer their students an opportunity to enroll in one or more dual enrollment courses.[28] These programs vary enormously, but research suggests that high school students who complete dual enrollment courses are more likely to complete college and graduate more quickly than other students.[29] For at least some types of students, dual enrollment courses can be an effective way to accumulate college credit and get a head start on college.

Many high school teachers and counselors encourage students to take dual enrollment classes because students only have to pass the course to receive college-level credit. In contrast, to earn credit by examination through an AP course, students must score sufficiently high on the AP exam, something many students are unable to do. And even when students do earn high scores on AP exams, the college they eventually attend may not always award CBE for the equivalent courses. Dual enrollment courses often therefore get promoted as a "sure" way to receive college credit from at least one college.

Before you enroll in a dual enrollment course at your high school, though, it's important to fully understand what you're getting yourself into. These are college courses, so expect them to be more challenging than your typical high school classes. Also be mindful that the grades you earn in dual enrollment courses become a permanent part of your university record and form part of your cumulative college GPA. That means that even if you took a dual enrollment course early in high school, your course grade may factor into the GPA that a business, law, or other graduate school will consider when you apply many years later. You should take a dual enrollment course only if you're fully prepared to invest the time and effort you need to get a good grade in it.

You also need to confirm that the university you plan to attend will award you credit hours toward your degree for any dual enrollment courses you complete. Many private universities refuse to award credit hours for dual enrollment classes, and policies at public universities vary widely. Some public universities don't award credit hours for every dual enrollment class, and even when they do, the credits might satisfy only an elective requirement, rather than general education or major requirements.

If your high school offers dual enrollment courses, make sure you get all the facts before you enroll. You don't want to find out later that your hard work doesn't pay off with credit hours at the university where you plan to earn your degree. And if you take a dual enrollment course, treat it like what it is: a college course, with a college grade, and all of a college grade's long-term consequences.

Strategic Advantages of Taking Transfer Courses

Using transfer courses as part of your degree completion strategy can benefit you in a number of ways. Here are some of them.

Graduate Early

Taking transfer courses provides you a potential opportunity to fulfill degree requirements ahead of schedule. As with credit by examination, if you earn transfer credit for enough courses, you may be able to graduate from college early.

Ensure Graduation in Four Years

Even if you don't want to graduate early, the credit hours you earn through transfer courses can help ensure that you graduate on time. As we've already discussed, most public university students take longer than four years to graduate. By taking transfer courses, you can get ahead on the course requirements you need to complete and reduce the risk that you won't graduate on time.

Complete Difficult Degree Requirements without Affecting Your Institutional GPA

If your university includes only its own course grades when it calculates your institutional GPA, you can fulfill course requirements in your weaker subjects or in otherwise problematic courses by taking them for transfer credit at other colleges—without putting your institutional GPA at risk. You get credit hours for the courses that count toward your degree, but no letter grades that affect your institutional GPA.

Even if your university does include the grades from transfer courses in your institutional GPA calculation, you can still benefit by taking certain classes at another college. If a particular class at your university is graded on a harsh curve, for example, you might be better off taking it for transfer credit at a different college where getting a high grade may be easier.

Take a Lighter Course Load

Taking courses at other colleges for transfer credit during the summer and then transferring the credit hours to your university can enable you to take a lighter course load during your regular semesters. This can leave you with more time to focus on doing well in the courses you do take.

A lighter course load also gives you room in your schedule to enrich your college experience outside of the classroom. You might, for example, get more involved in on-campus extracurricular activities or enjoy a more active social life than you would have with a heavier course load. As we discussed in Chapter 4, such activities aren't just fun. They can also be great ways to expand your skill set and build a strong network of professional and social contacts.

Gain Priority for Course Registration

As we discussed in Chapter 10, most public universities classify students as freshmen, sophomores, juniors, or seniors based on the number of credit hours they've completed, rather than on how long they've been in college. If you earn enough credit hours to be classified ahead of the students who began college at the same time you did, you may have priority over them, which entitles you to register for courses before they do. The credit hours you earn through transfer courses can help you do this. This priority for course registration helps lessen the risk that you will get stuck in undesirable courses, and it increases your chances of enrolling in the courses you want, taught by the professors you want.

Learning by Example

To show you how you might use transfer courses to your own advantage, here's the story of one public university student who benefited from taking transfer courses.

Aiden is a film studies major in his first semester at State University. After he graduates, he hopes to work in the film industry and eventually become a movie producer. The job market for this field is ultracompetitive, so Aiden wants to do everything he can to position himself well for his career—including compiling the highest institutional GPA he possibly can.

In high school, Aiden had a mixed academic record. He excelled in subjects with a strong writing and creative component, and he took a number of AP courses in them. However, he struggled just to get average grades in his math and natural science courses.

While in high school, Aiden managed to earn credit by examination (CBE) for seven courses at State University by scoring high enough on the AP or the corresponding CLEP exam. All of those courses fulfill general education course requirements. Although he took math and science CLEP exams in an attempt to earn CBE for math and natural science courses, he never earned a qualifying score.

Aiden's weakness in math and science posed a big problem for him. As part of Aiden's general education requirements, he must complete math and natural science distribution requirements consisting of a three-credit-hour math course and two four-credit-hour natural science courses. Furthermore, nearly all the introductory math and natural science courses at State University are graded on a strict curve. Many students consider these to be among the university's most notorious weed-out courses.

Acknowledging his weakness in math and science, Aiden looked for a way he might be able to fulfill those course requirements without putting his institutional GPA at risk. During the spring of his senior year in high school, he learned that State University does not average the grades from transfer courses into its students' institutional GPAs. He then made some inquiries.

First, Aiden learned exactly what math and natural sciences requirements he would have to fulfill at State University. He discovered that he had to take a math course at the level of pre-calculus or above, as well as two introductory courses in biology, chemistry, or physics. Since he took both biology and chemistry in high school, Aiden opted to satisfy his natural sciences requirement with introductory courses in those subjects. And given his weakness in math, Aiden not surprisingly chose pre-calculus, the lowest-level math class he could take to fulfill his math requirement.

Next, while he was still in high school, Aiden went online to get answers to the following questions:

- Does State University permit students to fulfill the math and natural science requirements with courses taken at Local Community College, the community college in Aiden's hometown?
- Does Local Community College offer transferable courses during the summer that could fulfill Aiden's math and natural sciences distribution requirements at State University?

Through his inquiries, Aiden learned that the answer to both questions was yes. But just to be sure, Aiden requested—and received—written confirmation via email from the registrar's office at State University that those courses at Local Community College would fulfill his degree requirements.

During the summer before his freshman year at State University, Aiden took pre-calculus, Introduction to Chemistry, and Introduction to Biology at Local Community College. The classes were not fun, but there was a silver lining: unlike in the equivalent courses at State University, the instructors at Local Community College did not grade on a curve. Further, each course had fewer than 30 students, so the format more closely resembled Aiden's high school classroom environment. Had he taken the equivalent classes at State University, they likely would have been taught in auditorium-size lecture halls.

After investing a lot of study time, Aiden managed to pull off a B in each course at Local Community College. Not stellar grades, but likely better than he would have earned at State University in those subjects.

By completing the three courses at Local Community College over the summer, what did Aiden accomplish in terms of satisfying requirements under his State University degree plan?

General Education Distribution	Degree Requirement	Aiden's Progress
Natural sciences	2 courses	By successfully completing Introduction to Biology and Introduction to Chemistry courses at Local Community College, he earned eight credit hours toward his degree and completed this entire distribution requirement. He doesn't need to take any natural sciences courses.
Mathematics	1 course	By successfully completing pre-calculus at Local Community College, he earned three credit hours toward his degree and completed this entire distribution requirement. He doesn't need to take any math courses.

Aside from fulfilling these requirements and earning a total of 11 credit hours toward his degree, by taking transfer courses at Local Community College, Aiden may benefit in the following additional ways:

- **Complete difficult degree requirements without affecting his institutional GPA.** The grades Aiden earned in the three courses at Local Community College will not affect his institutional GPA, since only classes taken at State University count toward his institutional GPA. Rather, Aiden will receive only credit hours from State University toward his degree, not letter grades.

  This is a good strategic move for Aiden. We know that Aiden had a lot of trouble academically in his math and natural science courses in high school. We also know that these courses at State University are graded on a strict curve and reputed to be weed-out courses. Had Aiden taken those courses at State University, they might have done lasting damage to his institutional GPA. But by taking these three courses for transfer credit at a different college, Aiden managed to fulfill potentially GPA-threatening degree plan requirements without any impact on his institutional GPA.

- **Graduate early and save a lot of money.** When he began his freshman year at State University, Aiden arrived with credit hours from these three transfer courses and seven courses for which he earned CBE. This is the equivalent of two full semesters—or an entire academic year—of his total required coursework. As a result, Aiden may be in a good position to complete his degree early and save a lot of time and money by doing so. Unlike many students who want to graduate early, Aiden won't necessarily have to take extra courses each semester— which could risk leaving him overwhelmed and limit his involvement in extracurricular and social activities.

- **Ensure he's able to graduate on time in four years.** Even if Aiden doesn't want to graduate early, the credit hours for the 10 courses that he earned through transfer credit and CBE have put him in a better position to graduate on time. He'll have more flexibility to take all the other courses he needs to finish in four years.

- **Take a lighter course load each semester.** Since Aiden began his freshman year at State University with 10 courses under his belt, he may be able to take a lighter course load each semester (if he doesn't want to graduate early). Doing this would allow Aiden to devote more time to doing well in each of the courses he does take.

  A lighter course load may also give Aiden more time to participate in social and extracurricular activities—in addition to the activities he could have comfortably managed with a heavier course load. These activities aren't necessarily just enjoyable; well-chosen activities can greatly broaden both his skill set and his potential network of contacts, which can provide Aiden an edge when he applies for internships and jobs.

- **Have priority for course registration over the other students who started with him.** Thanks to the transfer courses he completed over the summer and the CBE he earned, Aiden arrived at State

University with more than a year's worth of credit hours. When it's time to register for his second-semester courses there, State University will likely classify him as a sophomore. As a result, he should be able to register before his classmates who remain classified as freshmen. This may enable Aiden to register for more of his first-choice courses and professors.

- **Focus on courses that will benefit his future plans.** Because Aiden fulfilled so many of his general education course requirements through transfer coursework and CBE, he can focus his studies more on courses that interest him in his major and other related subject areas. Since Aiden wants to eventually be a film producer, he might use the time in his schedule to take additional courses in film studies sooner. Or, given the importance of financial savvy on the production side of the film business, perhaps he could add a minor in finance or accounting. Gaining these or other skills can make Aiden a more desirable candidate when he applies for internships and jobs.

Potential Pitfalls of Transfer Coursework

Fulfilling requirements under your degree plan with transfer courses can offer you a lot of advantages. However, it doesn't always make sense to do this. Let's look at a couple of strategic mistakes some students make when they take transfer courses, and discuss other potential downsides to using transfer courses as part of your degree completion strategy. Once you are aware of them, you can avoid making these types of strategic errors.

Not Strategically Selecting the Courses to Take for Transfer Credit

Many students don't think strategically about what courses to take at other colleges for transfer credit. Don't make this mistake. Always have a good reason for taking a course at a different college.

For example, you might take a transfer course because the equivalent course at your university would likely be harder, thus jeopardizing your institutional GPA. Or, because you are lousy in math, you might take your required math courses at a different college where the grades you earn won't get averaged into your institutional GPA. Those would both be good reasons. After all, you want to minimize your potential risks from courses that stand a good chance of lowering your institutional GPA, and a strategic approach using transfer courses can help you do this.

Be aware, though, of situations in which taking a transfer course could hurt your institutional GPA by not improving it. Let's assume, for example, that your university includes only its course grades when it calculates your institutional GPA. If you would be likely to earn a grade in a course at your university that would improve your institutional GPA, you probably shouldn't take the equivalent course at a different college for transfer credit. You'd be giving up a good opportunity to improve your institutional GPA by taking that course at your university. Remember: if your goal is to maximize your institutional GPA, you should take courses at other colleges for transfer credit only if you have a good reason to do so.

Taking Transfer Courses Before Attempting to Earn CBE

Many students take the wrong strategic approach when they don't explore the possibility of earning CBE before they take a course for transfer credit. Always find out if you can earn CBE for courses before you enroll in them. If you can't earn CBE instead, fine—at least you've checked. But if CBE is a possibility and you feel you have at least some chance of passing the exam and earning CBE, give CBE a shot. In most instances, you have much to gain, and little to lose, by trying to earn CBE first.

Some Universities Average Grades from Transfer Courses into the Institutional GPA

When a majority of public universities calculate the institutional GPA of their students, they exclude the grades from courses taken at most other colleges. However, some universities do include all or nearly all university-level grades in this calculation. Still others may consider them solely to determine eligibility for graduation with GPA-based honors. Since this varies, it's important to know your university's transfer course policy inside and out.

If you attend a university that does include the grades from transfer courses in your institutional GPA, you will need to alter your approach. Merely taking your difficult courses for transfer credit at other colleges won't protect your institutional GPA. It can still be useful, however, to take what would be difficult, weed-out, or harshly graded courses at your university at a different college with more relaxed grading standards or lower admission standards. If you attend the public university with the highest admission standards in your state, for example, it may be easier to get the high grades you want at a different college that admits all students; you may have less competition there.

Grades from Transfer Courses Always Count Toward Your Cumulative GPA

Graduate schools almost always look at your cumulative GPA when they consider you for admission. This gives you a major incentive to do your best in all your courses, regardless of where you take them. But it's also a sobering reminder of why you should usually seek to fulfill difficult degree requirements through CBE whenever you have the opportunity.

Let's say you take Introduction to Biology at the community college in your hometown during a summer break and earn a C. While your university might not include that grade in its calculation of your institutional GPA, the grade still figures into your cumulative GPA.

Every graduate school you apply to will likely see that C on your transcript and take it into account for admissions purposes.

On the other hand, if you pass the CLEP Biology exam with a score equivalent to a grade of C, as long as your university will award CBE for a passing score, you earn "Credit," but no letter grade. There's no record of your unimpressive exam score on your transcript; it likely just states you received credit for the course. It has no impact whatsoever on your institutional GPA or your cumulative GPA.

Because transfer courses get included in your cumulative GPA, attempt to fulfill degree plan requirements through CBE first if your university offers that option—and if you feel you have at least some chance of passing. After all, you have nothing to lose by trying to earn CBE, and you may be pleasantly surprised when you succeed.

Learning by Example

Here's the story of a public university freshman who didn't take a strategic approach to choosing which courses to take for transfer credit or to exploring his options to fulfill course requirements through CBE.

Jake, a computer science major at State University, is midway through his first semester. In high school, he excelled in math and science courses but struggled in writing-intensive courses like English, U.S. history, and government. Writing essays and term papers has never come easy for Jake.

To get a head start on fulfilling his degree requirements, Jake took two college courses at Local Community College the summer before his freshman year. Because he didn't want to make his summer miserable by taking courses that would require a lot of writing, Jake took two courses in subjects that were easy for him in high school: Calculus I and Introduction to Chemistry.

Before taking these courses, Jake received written confirmation from State University that each had an equivalent course there for which he could receive transfer credit toward his degree. Unfortunately, he didn't ask whether he might be able to earn CBE for those courses. Had Jake done so, he would have learned that State University also allows students to earn CBE for each of those courses through CLEP exams.

Jake took both courses over the summer at Local Community College, earning an A in each one. However, since State University includes only its own course grades in its institutional GPA calculation, neither of those As were averaged into Jake's institutional GPA.

At his freshman orientation at State University, Jake registered for his courses for the fall semester. The classes he signed up for included English Composition and U.S. History to 1877, two required courses with heavy writing components.

Now, after learning his midterm averages in his English composition and U.S. history courses, Jake is afraid that he may not get a passing final grade in either of them.

Had Jake thought more strategically before taking his courses at Local Community College last summer, he could have avoided the situation he finds himself in. He made several strategic errors.

First, Jake didn't explore his options to earn CBE. This was a critical mistake. Instead of spending his summer at community college and his fall struggling through two difficult classes, he could have first tried to earn CBE for all four of those courses. Had he been able to squeak by with a score just high enough to earn CBE at State University, he would have received credit for those courses without having to take them at all. For some or all of these courses, he might have saved himself both tuition and time by earning CBE.

Second, Jake took the wrong courses for transfer credit. Because State University includes only its own course grades in its institutional GPA calculation, the two As he earned at Local Community College don't improve his institutional GPA. He missed a potential opportunity to bolster his institutional GPA by taking those courses at State University, where he might have earned high grades in both. The courses he should have taken at Local Community College were English composition and U.S. history (assuming he didn't earn CBE for them instead). Even if Jake had earned below-average grades in those courses, the grades still wouldn't have affected his institutional GPA at State University.

Unfortunately, Jake now finds himself stuck taking two writing-intensive courses. He's created a tough slog for himself, as well as a potential GPA-crushing situation. The fact that he did well in his first college-level courses at Local Community College may have been a confidence-booster, but those courses did nothing for his institutional GPA at State University. Jake's failure to think strategically about how he fulfills his course requirements may now hurt his long-term GPA prospects.

Don't be like Jake. Always think strategically.

Getting to Know Yourself

Too many students don't pay enough attention to the most important determinant of their success in college: themselves. This causes them to make easily avoidable mistakes when picking their courses. They take classes that are ill suited to them in many ways, ranging from the course subject to the way a class is structured and graded.

For you to effectively develop a university game plan and select courses that can help maximize your GPA, you need to think carefully about your academic strengths and weaknesses and the course structure and grading format that best position you to do well in your courses. In Part V, we show you what factors to take into account in making these determinations.

By the end of Part V, you'll be better positioned to take yourself into account whenever you choose courses.

Know Yourself as a Student: GPAMaxx Cardinal Rule #2

This Chapter Covers

- Identifying your academic strengths and weaknesses
- Identifying your preferred format for courses

Most of us are left-handed or right-handed. We're wired with this predisposition from birth. We have more natural aptitude with one hand than the other. If we're right-handed, we likely throw a baseball and sign our name with our right hand. Even if we practiced these activities all day using our left hand, we probably wouldn't become more skilled with our left hand than our right. We wouldn't throw the baseball or sign our name better left-handed. Sure, we could improve with practice, repetition, and hard work, but we'd be fighting our natural tendencies the entire time.

For most students, college academics work the same way. You have more natural aptitude and greater strength in some areas than in others. Some subjects come more easily to you; some are harder. The same holds true for your learning style. You learn more effectively in some types of courses than in others. You may learn better in a small group where you constantly interact and engage with others than in a giant lecture hall amidst a sea of other students where you just listen. And when it comes to how you get graded on your work, you tend to do better on some types of assignments than on others. Writing essay exams may come much more easily to you than answering multiple-choice questions, or vice versa.

Ideally, you want to select courses in subjects that play to your strengths and are taught in a way that meshes well with your learning style, with instructors who determine grades based on types of work that you naturally find easier. When you select courses that meet those conditions, you position yourself for success from the outset. You may still have to put in a lot of work to get the grades you want, but you've set the stage to do well.

The catch: before you can find courses that fit well, you need to know yourself as a student. This self-awareness comes primarily not from a gut feeling, but from carefully looking at your past performance. This is the idea behind GPAMaxx Cardinal Rule #2: *Know Yourself as a Student*.

Unfortunately, many students lack this kind of self-awareness and set themselves up for a bad outcome when they register for their courses. Instead of choosing courses that are a good fit for them, given their unique strengths, weaknesses, and preferences, they often do the exact opposite. They select courses that are wrong for them in every respect, from the subject matter to the format of the course to the way they'll be graded. These poor choices often have lasting consequences on their GPAs and close off opportunities they might have had after graduation.

Don't let this happen to you. To position yourself to succeed academically, it's important to learn just what kind of student you are.

Getting to Know Yourself as a Student: Necessary Steps

To know yourself as a student, you need to determine the following:

- Your academic strengths and weaknesses
- Your preferred format for coursework

When you understand these things, you can put yourself in a much better position to choose courses that are conducive to your academic success and a high GPA.

Identify Your Academic Strengths and Weaknesses

If you're like most of us, you aren't great at everything. That includes some of the subjects that your college requires you to study. You have an aptitude for and excel in some subjects, but you're only average in a few others. Maybe you're just plain lousy in one or two subjects. Unfortunately, too many students spend excessive time and hurt their academic records trying to fix their weaknesses rather than making the most of their strengths. As a result, they don't shine academically.

The solution: instead of trying to transform yourself and ace your weaker subjects, focus on your strengths to the fullest extent possible, and find ways to minimize or eliminate the impact of your weaknesses on your GPA.

To do this, you need a realistic awareness of your academic strengths: general subject areas and disciplines where you're at your strongest and possess the most aptitude. You also need to identify and accept your academic weaknesses: general subject areas and disciplines where you're at your weakest.

Discovering your academic strengths and weaknesses empowers you. With this self-awareness, you can better select your courses to maximize the impact of your strengths, and minimize or even completely eliminate the impact of your weaknesses. You can look for ways to take more courses in your strong subjects and fewer in your weaker ones. And if you do have to take courses in your weaker subjects, you can find ways to do so that won't affect your institutional GPA.

Determine Your Preferred Format

Too many students underestimate the importance of selecting courses that are structured in a way that facilitates their academic success. Many students completely ignore courses' formats when they register each semester. They simply don't give a thought to how a course is set up and how they will be graded.

This isn't surprising. Universities themselves rarely emphasize how important it is for students to pay attention to a class's format when they choose their courses.

Far too often, students are midway through the semester when they realize they're enrolled in a course with a format that's completely wrong for them. They prefer essay exams, term papers, class discussions, and small class sizes. But as if they're in a bad dream, they find themselves with 499 other students in an auditorium-size course taught by a professor they may never meet, who grades on a harsh curve based solely on the results of three multiple-choice exams. By then it's usually too late. There's a GPA train wreck coming—and it's coming fast!

If you choose courses in your preferred format, you can better avoid these kinds of unpleasant surprises.

Your **preferred format** is the way your ideal course would be structured—essentially, your dream course structure. Courses taught in your preferred format offer the kind of classroom experience you'd like to have, taught and structured the way you learn most effectively, and graded in just the way you like to be evaluated for your performance. Obviously, you won't be able to take every course in your preferred format. Some semesters it may be hard to find any courses in your preferred format. That's okay. Your preferred format should be the yardstick by which you measure all the courses you consider.

Your preferred format consists of two components: your ideal instructional format and your ideal grading format.

Your Ideal Instructional Format

Your **ideal instructional format** is the type of classroom environment in which you learn most effectively. Just as most of us have academic strengths and weaknesses, most of us learn better in some learning environments than in others.

You might thrive in small classes where you constantly interact with your classmates and instructor, but feel intimidated and disengaged in giant auditorium-size courses where the instructor has no idea who you are. One of your friends, on the other hand, might prefer to blend into the mass of students in lecture halls and feel out of his element and tongue-tied in smaller courses and seminars. Some of us need a personal connection to our instructors, while others prefer to learn more independently.

Because we're all different, our ideal instructional formats can vary widely. The one thing that remains the same is that we're more likely to succeed and thrive academically in courses where the learning environment suits us.

That's why you should always try to narrow your list of potential courses to those taught in your ideal instructional format, or as close to it as possible. A perfect match won't always exist, but try to come as close as you can.

Timing Is Everything

As you determine your preferred format, you should also consider the time of day when the class meets. Taking a lot of early-morning classes so you can have your afternoons free may seem like a good idea when you're registering for courses. However, once the semester starts, many students find themselves regularly sleeping through early-morning classes.

This isn't necessarily the case with every student. But without Mom and Dad around to make them go to school, many students find the appeal of sleeping late more enticing than any history or biology class. Unless you know you're a morning person, you may want to err on the side of caution and avoid early-morning courses.

Your Ideal Grading Format

The way your instructor determines your final grade in a class can vary enormously from course to course, and from instructor to instructor. One instructor might base your final grade solely on a couple of multiple-choice exams, while another instructor teaching the same course might base final grades on the results of three essay exams and two term papers. To increase your chances of success, you want to select courses that give the most weight to the types of coursework at which you excel.

The **grading format** of a course is the mixture of exams, homework, term papers, class participation, and other variables that the instructor uses to determine each student's final course grade. Your **ideal grading format** is how you, given a choice, want to have your grade determined. If you're especially good at writing papers and taking essay exams, you'd want your grade based primarily on your work on those activities. If you do better on multiple-choice tests, on the other hand, you'd want your grade based on how you do on them.

The grading format can have a huge effect on your performance in a course, so it's important to focus on it. Always try to find courses that closely—if not perfectly—match your ideal grading format.

In Chapter 13, we'll show you several things you can do to determine your ideal instructional and grading formats.

Don't Forget to Consider a Course's Workload

Whenever you evaluate a course's suitability, think about its probable workload. Even if you like the way a potential course's grade gets determined, that course can be a nonstarter for you if it would require a disproportionate amount of work compared to your other classes. Say, for example, that a course requires you to submit lengthy weekly essays that count as a significant percentage of your final grade. The fact that you like to write and have an aptitude for it might not outweigh the fact that you simply won't have time in your schedule to write really good essays every week.

A disproportionately heavy workload in one course can force you to pull your most valuable resource—your time—away from your other courses, causing your grades in them to suffer. Getting an A in the course with the heavy workload, but ending up with Bs in all the others as a result, shows poor strategic planning. Think about the big picture. Always keep the likely workload in mind when determining whether a course is a good fit for you.

CHAPTER

13

Finding Your Inner Student

This Chapter Covers

- Determining your academic strengths and weaknesses
- Discovering your preferred format

After the last chapter, you may be scratching your head. Getting to know yourself as a student isn't always easy. We wouldn't be surprised if you don't immediately recognize your academic strengths and weaknesses or know right away what course format is best for you.

If that's the case, you have plenty of company. This kind of self-analysis is tough for a lot of students, especially those who got very good grades in high school but don't have experience in college courses yet. If you're one of those students, don't let your unfamiliarity with college classes put your GPA at risk. You need to do some legwork to minimize the risk of making poor course choices.

In this chapter, we show you ways to make these sometimes difficult self-evaluations on your own.

Determining Your Academic Strengths and Weaknesses

You don't need to psychoanalyze yourself to get a good idea of the subjects in which you are strong and weak. A couple of straightforward evaluations can help determine your academic strengths and weaknesses.

Let Experience Guide You

Many college courses, especially general education and introductory courses, cover the same subjects as classes offered in high school. It makes sense to leverage your high school experiences—both good and bad—to help you select your courses.

If you had trouble with a particular subject in high school, you're unlikely to find it magically easier in college. It will still be a tough subject for you. All too often, however, new college students don't learn from experience when they register for their courses. Many of them enroll in courses in the same subjects that gave them problems in high school.

Don't be one of those students. Draw from your experience in high school to develop an awareness of your own academic strengths and weaknesses. Use that knowledge to help determine which courses are a good fit for you. And find ways to fulfill course requirements in your weaker subjects in ways that won't affect your institutional GPA.

To do this effectively, you'll need to think about your strengths and weaknesses carefully. Making a table like Table 13–1 can help you do this. It is a simple tool, but actually going through the process can help you enormously.

Table 13-1

High School Subject	Strength	Weakness	Neutral

In the first column of Table 13–1, make a list of all the subjects you took in high school. Include all the core subjects, like English, chemistry, biology, algebra, pre-calculus, American history, and American government, as well as any electives.

Next, think about which of those subjects are your areas of strength. Often, these are the courses in which you did well in high school and earned a good grade without trying too hard. It may also be helpful to look back at your scores on the various sections of the standardized college admissions exams, like the ACT and the SAT. Talking with your parents is another good idea. You will likely recognize some subjects immediately as ones for which you have some aptitude. Put a check in the "Strength" column in Table 13–1 for those subjects.

Determining your strengths can be tricky, so think about these subjects carefully. You can't always judge strictly by the grade you earned in a particular course. It's entirely possible that you earned a good grade in a certain class even though it was hard for you. Maybe you got an A in high school calculus not because you have an aptitude for it, but because your teacher was a notoriously easy grader or was willing to spend extra time explaining things to you. If you found the material in high school calculus difficult, you wouldn't want to classify it as one of your academic strengths even if you got an A after much hard work.

When it comes to selecting your university courses, especially in your first few semesters, you should be cautious about subjects that you don't immediately recognize as strengths. You want to get off to a good start at college academically; the last thing you need in your first semester is a course that poses a high risk of hurting your GPA right from the get-go. If you have any real doubts about whether a subject plays to your strengths, put a check in the "Neutral" column of Table 13–1.

Once you determine the subjects you consider to be your academic strengths, it's time to turn to your weaknesses. As you did with your strengths, put a check in the "Weakness" column of Table 13–1 next to any subject for which you lack aptitude or must work hard just to achieve a mediocre or even disappointing result. Again, you may find it helpful to look at your high school grades, review your performance on standardized tests, and talk with your parents.

As you do your analysis, you may find that some subjects are neither strengths nor weaknesses for you. Put those in the "Neutral" column, and proceed cautiously with university courses in those subjects.

By going through this exercise, you can get at least some sense of your potential academic strengths and weaknesses, as well as the areas in which you feel yourself to be only average. When you develop your university game plan and pick your courses, you want to take this information into account.

Use Available Resources to Investigate Each Potential University Subject Before You Register for Courses

Today more than ever, there are lots of ways to find out about particular subjects and whether they play to your strengths or weaknesses.

First, check the internet. Numerous websites let you view videos of an entire semester's worth of recorded lectures from previously held university courses. Watch a few lectures that cover the same subject as a course that you may want to take. Look as well at the related course materials available online. Doing this can give you a sense of whether the course topic interests you and whether you might have some aptitude for it.

In addition to using online resources, if you're already enrolled at your university, sit in on a couple of lectures in the course you may take in the future. If it's an auditorium-size lecture course, you can probably slip in with the other students without anyone even noticing you. For smaller classes, tell the instructor you might take the course in a future semester and want to get a feel for it. Many instructors will be receptive to your interest.

Once you have a general idea of whether a subject plays to your strengths or your weaknesses, look at the syllabus for any course you might take. A syllabus usually lays out the objectives and goals of a course, an outline of the topics to be covered, a schedule, and a description of how the instructor determines grades.

Many instructors post a course syllabus or description online prior to registration. If that isn't the case at your university, or if nothing's been posted for a course that interests you, you might have to email the instructor and request that she send it to you. Either way, you must take the initiative to inform yourself.

Discovering Your Preferred Format: Your Ideal Instructional and Grading Formats

For many of you, discovering your preferred format may be just as difficult as pinpointing your academic strengths and weaknesses, for several reasons.

First, you may not have a clear sense of your ideal grading format, one of the two components that make up your preferred format. We discussed these components in detail in Chapter 12. This is especially true for those of you who haven't started college. High school courses are often graded much more leniently than university ones, and many college freshmen have no idea what format works best for them. They're used to getting good grades in every high school grading format, from essay and short-answer exams to term papers to homework to multiple-choice tests.

Their high school success leaves many new college students with no clear sense of their ideal grading format. That causes them to take courses with formats that turn out to be a poor fit. The result: many go from having been straight-A multiple-choice test takers in high school to average or even below-average ones at college. For those of you who performed much better in high school in some types of grading formats than in others, that can be a big advantage in college. Your experience may leave you with a clearer sense of your ideal grading format.

Second, especially if you haven't started college yet, you just may not have the experience to determine what constitutes your ideal instructional format. You certainly can't say you don't learn well in auditorium-size lecture courses if you've never sat through one. If you've never taken a small seminar class, you don't know what that's like, either. You have to test the waters during your initial semesters at college to find out what constitutes your ideal instructional format. The trick is to do this without endangering your GPA.

Reducing the Risk of Taking Courses in Unsuitable Formats for You

There are a few things you can do to minimize the risk of choosing courses that are ill suited to your ideal instructional and grading formats.

Research the Format of Any Course You Consider

First, check out the grading and instructional formats of each potential course. Before you do anything else, get the course syllabus and read it carefully. You might not know exactly what type of classroom experience constitutes your ideal learning format, but you may have at least some sense of your ideal grading format, so pay special attention to how the instructor determines the course grade.

If you excelled at writing essay exams and term papers but struggled with multiple-choice tests in high school, you'd likely want to select courses in which your grade depends on term papers and essay exams rather than on multiple-choice tests. If you're shy and hardly uttered a word in your high school classes, taking a course in which class participation makes up a significant portion of your final grade probably wouldn't be a good idea.

You get the picture. By actively seeking out the grading format that will allow you to shine in your coursework, you can both head off potential problems before they arise and set the stage for success in your courses.

Try to Take Courses in Familiar Instructional Formats

To find out your ideal instructional format, you have to experience different course formats for yourself. That doesn't mean you simply take the plunge and enroll in courses with formats that are new to you; you want to do things cautiously, on your own terms.

Be just as careful about unfamiliar instructional formats as you are with unfamiliar subjects when you pick your courses. As we mentioned, if you haven't started college, you probably haven't experienced the auditorium-size lecture courses that are, unfortunately, commonplace at public universities, particularly in general education and some introductory courses.

Rather than registering for a series of auditorium-size lecture courses for your first semester, look for alternatives in a format closer to the kind of classes you took in high school. Many universities offer courses in a variety of instructional formats that fulfill the same degree plan requirement, so you can often seek out those courses taught in more familiar formats. For example, to fulfill the social sciences course requirement under your degree plan, a 15-student Introduction to Cultural Geography freshman seminar might be a better option than the auditorium-size Introduction to Psychology. If you can't avoid enrolling in auditorium-size courses entirely, try to take as few as possible.

Essentially, you want to dip your toes in the course selection waters to see how well you respond to different instructional formats without putting your GPA at risk. By proceeding cautiously, you minimize the risk.

The Best Course for Your GPA Might Be the One You Don't Take

We know that our suggestions are not foolproof. Going through the exercises in this chapter is no guarantee you won't have difficulty with a subject that you thought was going to be easy, or that you won't do poorly in a course taught in a format that you like. The demands of college-level courses are entirely different from those of high school classes, and no book or program can guarantee a good grade.

Rather, we've made these suggestions to prompt you to think about these types of issues when you select your courses. Remember the lingering effect that a single bad grade can have on your GPA. The best course for your GPA might therefore be the one you don't take. If our approach keeps you from taking even one course that might have lowered your GPA significantly, you'll be very glad you spent the time doing this analysis.

The "Like" Factor in Choosing Your Courses

Throughout Part V, we've stressed the importance of finding courses that play to your strengths and are taught in your preferred format. However, just because a course meets those criteria doesn't mean you'll necessarily like it or that it will interest you.

Say that English is your strongest subject. That doesn't mean that you'll like all English courses or even find them interesting. You might have no interest in poetry, for example. If that's the case, whenever you have other courses to choose from, avoid any course that focuses on poetry. Instead, search for an alternate course that fulfills the same requirement and seems to be a better fit for you.

This may seem like common sense. However, all too often, students register for a course that they're pretty sure they won't like, even when they have several other courses to choose from. Frequently you may not have any other choice than to take a particular course. But when you do have options, think long and hard before you take a course that doesn't interest you, even if it's in your preferred format and in a general subject area that you like. If the topic of a course doesn't interest you at all, it can be harder for you to do well in it, no matter what else the course has going for it. In addition to seeking out courses in your strongest subject areas and your preferred format, always keep the "like" factor in mind.

Learning to Professor Shop

Selecting university courses that help you shine academically and win at the GPA game requires a balance of multiple considerations. As we discussed in Part V, it's critical to find courses that play to your strengths and are taught in your preferred format. That's the first part of the equation. The second part is finding instructors who offer you the best chances of getting high grades. You can accomplish this second part by professor shopping, the subject of Part VI.

Professor shopping is the process through which you discover how instructors have previously graded their students in a course. Because instructors often grade the same courses the same way year after year, professor shopping will allow you to get a sense of how they might grade you before you register for their classes. Once you have a sense of how instructors previously graded students in your potential course, you can take this information into account when you select the courses that are the best fit for you and your GPA.

After you read Part VI, you'll understand how to find the instructors who generally award the highest grades in your potential courses.

14

Know How to Professor Shop: GPAMaxx Cardinal Rule #3

This Chapter Covers

- The basics of professor shopping

Let's imagine once again that you are at your university's freshman orientation. It's almost time to register for your first semester, and you are deciding which courses to take. You are looking at a course that fulfills a general education requirement. The course has three separate sections, each of which is taught in your preferred format. You like how the course is structured and how your grade will be determined in each section.

Three instructors teach separate sections of this course. The first and second are drill sergeant graders; you learn that there were a disproportionate number of low grades in past semesters in each of their sections. However, the third instructor appears to be a much more measured grader. Over the past four semesters, this instructor has always given a disproportionately larger percentage of As and Bs to students enrolled in her section than the other two instructors have.

Since the course format is the same in each section of the course, if you're like most students, you'd probably want to take the course with the third instructor, the one who seems most likely to offer the best chances to earn a high grade. Before you can choose the instructor who will likely grade most favorably, though, you'd have to learn how to find her.

The principle behind GPAMaxx Cardinal Rule #3: *Know How to Professor Shop* is simple: knowing how to analyze your potential university instructors based on their past grading practices and tendencies can help you find the instructor and course most likely to be a GPA winner for you.

Professor shopping is the process through which you can discover how instructors have previously graded students in a particular course. At many universities, it's possible to learn the exact percentage breakdown of As, Bs, Cs, Ds, and Fs an instructor awarded in previous semesters. Any time you can identify instructors who may be likelier to be grade-friendly, you can use that information to your strategic advantage.

Knowing How an Instructor Previously Graded Can Help You

Instructors' grading patterns are often fairly consistent. They tend to give similar grades in the same types of courses semester after semester, year after year. A drill sergeant grader stays a drill sergeant, while measured graders stay measured. By learning how an instructor distributed grades in a particular course during past semesters, you can get a sense of how he or she may grade that same class in the future.

Be aware, though, that you won't always be able to uncover this kind of information for all—or even a majority—of your potential courses. Sometimes the grade distribution histories of instructors for past semesters won't be available at all. But whenever you can access this information, professor shopping can be a great strategic tool.

In those instances, once you find courses taught in your preferred format (using the principles from GPAMaxx Cardinal Rule #2: *Know Yourself as a Student*), you can narrow down your list of potential courses even further by finding out which instructors teaching those courses have graded most favorably in the past.

Professor Shopping: A Case Study

Make no mistake—researching the past grade distributions of individual instructors takes some effort on your part. But don't be tempted to skip professor shopping. It's well worth your time and effort. Discovering an instructor's grading patterns can be invaluable in identifying courses that have a higher likelihood of being GPA winners for you.

Let's look at a real-life example of how significantly grade distributions can vary, even in the same course taught in the same semester. Below is the final grade breakdown for the three instructors who taught a history course, The United States from 1865 to the Present, at a large public university in the South during a single semester. The charts show the grades each instructor awarded for the same course during the same semester. As you can see, the variation in the grade distributions—in particular, the difference in the percentage of As each instructor awarded—is amazing.

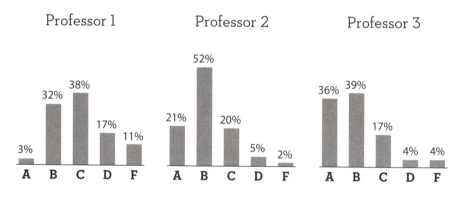

What does this example demonstrate? First and foremost, it shows the often-dramatic differences in grading practices of instructors who teach the same course during the exact same semester. Without multiple semesters of data, though, you still need to be cautious about drawing too many conclusions about each instructor's grading history. For example, Professor 3 may have had a disproportionately bright group of students in this one semester, while Professor 1 may have taught a particularly average bunch of students. But this real-life example highlights the need to understand how potential instructors graded a course in the past, given that they may grade similarly in the future.

Don't Select Your Courses Based Only on Professor Shopping

Professor shopping can help you select the most suitable instructor, but don't pick your instructors based solely on how they graded students in the past. This is just one of multiple factors you need to consider. Even after you professor shop and find an instructor with very favorable past grade distributions, there can be good reasons not to take her course. For example, if she isn't teaching it in your preferred format, you may be better off taking the course with an instructor who does, even if that instructor is a tougher grader.

Often you must weigh competing factors when choosing your classes. In Chapter 17, we show you how you can use professor shopping as part of your larger analysis to help pick the courses that are the best fit for you and your GPA.

Professor Shopping: A Tutorial

This Chapter Covers

- Steps to professor shopping
- Four tips for effective professor shopping
- Questions to ask yourself every time you professor shop

Now that we have introduced GPAMaxx Cardinal Rule #3: *Know How to Professor Shop*, you understand how professor shopping can potentially help you. This chapter takes things a step further and shows you how to professor shop on your own.

Steps to Professor Shop

Professor shopping consists of four steps:

1. **Locate grade distribution histories of each instructor for the course in which you are interested.**

   Before you do anything else, you need to obtain the grade distribution histories of each instructor whose course you want to analyze. You can't professor shop without them.

   The best way to obtain an instructor's grade distribution history depends in large part on your university. Some universities provide access to them, but most don't. If your university doesn't, you need to turn to the internet.

A number of websites make databases available that break down instructors' grade distributions in specific courses, semester by semester. One of the best known is www.koofers.com. At present, it is free and contains grade distribution histories for thousands of instructors and their courses, as well as vast amounts of other information that may be of interest to you. This website may be a good starting point for your professor shopping.

Since none of the websites currently available to students contains complete grade distribution information for every university, you may need to check several sites. It's also a good idea to talk with other students at your university to see if they have suggestions for the best sites covering your school.

2. **Review the grade distribution histories of each instructor for the specific course.**

If you can find the grade distribution histories of each instructor for the course you wish to analyze, you need to review each instructor's patterns separately.

For example, if you're considering Introduction to Macroeconomics with Professor Aguilar, you want to look at her grade distributions for each semester in which she has taught that specific course. Don't expect to find information for every semester, or that her grade distributions will be the same in every semester. Professor shopping is not an exact science. You want a general sense of Professor Aguilar's grading tendencies. Does it appear that she usually grades this course on a strict curve? Does she seem to be more of a measured grader? These are the types of things you want to look for whenever you analyze an instructor.

When you review the grade distribution histories of different instructors, it's easy to get them confused. Make sure you record your findings for each instructor separately.

3. **Compare the grade distribution histories of each instructor teaching the course.**

Now that you have information about all the instructors, compare them with one another. Try to get a sense of which instructor appears to grade students most favorably.

4. **Weigh the grading history information along with other data, including course format, to help you choose the best course for you.**

In Step 3, you may have been able to get a sense of which instructor seems likely to grade most favorably. But that might not be the most important consideration for you. You need to balance this information against the format of the course before you make a final decision.

In some cases, you may give greater weight to the fact that an instructor will determine your grade through the types of coursework in which you excel, even if the instructor isn't the most favorable grader. For example, if you write great term papers but don't generally do as well on multiple-choice exams, you might be better off taking the course in which term papers make up your entire grade—even if the instructor generally grades more harshly and awards a lower percentage of As than one who gives only multiple-choice exams.

Now that you know the basic steps, you're almost ready to professor shop on your own. Before you start, though, there are a few things you need to watch out for.

Five Tips for Effective Professor Shopping

Below are five tips you need to keep in mind whenever you professor shop. If you don't consider them, you risk misinterpreting grade distribution histories and drawing flawed conclusions about an instructor's grading tendencies.

1. **Always check an instructor's grade distribution histories in a particular course over several semesters when that information is available.**

   An instructor's grade distribution history in a particular semester may misrepresent his actual grading tendencies for many reasons. Maybe a cheating scandal resulted in a large number of poor grades during a particular semester. In another semester, he might have had a very small class consisting of students who were all quite strong academically and earned atypically high grades as a result.

   Whenever possible, you want to analyze more than one semester of an instructor's grade breakdowns. This increases the likelihood that past grade distributions are representative rather than flukes.

2. **Start your research by looking at the past grade distribution histories of the instructor only in the particular course you may take.**

   Learning about an instructor's grade history and the average GPA for all the courses she teaches is of no use. Such extraneous information can, in fact, be completely misleading.

   Instructors may award grades differently depending on the type of course. For example, they may have one way of grading auditorium-size introductory and general education courses for freshmen, and another for a small seminar course geared to upper-division students. An instructor may grade far more leniently when teaching an introductory or general education course open only to freshmen in the university honors program than she would in a course open to all students.

To professor shop effectively, therefore, you must obtain the grade distributions for the exact course you plan to take. If that information isn't available, you want to look at a course in a similar format, aimed at a similar level and type of student.

Unfortunately, some websites that claim to provide a breakdown of instructors' past grade distributions don't do so on a course-by-course basis. Instead, they provide only the average GPA and the instructors' grade distributions across all the courses they teach.

That information is virtually useless. After all, if you hope to take a 15-student freshman seminar, you won't learn much about the instructor from a breakdown of grade distributions across all the courses she's taught in previous semesters, including 250-student auditorium-size lecture courses. In fact, the available data will likely mislead you.

Always keep in mind when professor shopping that you must tailor your search to the specific course you may take, or one very similar to it.

3. **When an instructor hasn't taught a course previously, only grade distribution histories of courses taught in similar formats aimed at similarly situated students will likely be helpful.**

You may encounter instances in which an instructor teaches a course for the first time. In that case, no grading history exists for you to analyze. This complicates your analysis, but you aren't completely out of luck. You now need to check whether any grade distribution histories are available for that instructor for similar courses. In determining what makes a course similar, the subject matter is largely irrelevant. Instead, you want to focus on the course format and the type of student who typically takes the course.

Say you want to research the grading history of a professor who is teaching a 20-student freshman seminar for the first time next semester. To do so, you want to analyze other freshman seminars the professor has taught. The professor's grade distributions in a course geared to a different type of student may not be a reliable indicator, so try to find ones that fit a similar profile.

4. **When you have access to an instructor's grade distribution histories, do not give much weight to what you read in student evaluations or in online forums.**

The instructor ratings and comments in student evaluations and online are called anecdotal information because they draw on observations and personal stories and experiences. For a number of reasons, anecdotal information is far less useful to you than information based on facts and figures, such as an instructor's grading history. And in some cases, using anecdotal information can do more harm than good, clouding the information you already have.

The website www.ratemyprofessors.com is among the best known of the college professor and course tell-all websites, but others exist, including some that are specific to particular universities.

A central problem with the anecdotal information on these websites is the source. Usually, the instructor ratings and the related comments come solely from students who voluntarily share their thoughts and opinions.

Often, these students are not representative of the entire class. Rather, they may represent only the far ends of the spectrum. On the one hand, there are students with an ax to grind. Maybe they didn't like their final grades or had some other problem with the instructor or course. At the other extreme are the students who sing the praises of the instructor. Maybe they aced the course or have some other reason for being so positive. Between the two extremes lie the majority of students—the ones who never bother to comment. Because you don't get the opinions of this usually very large silent majority, you can easily get an inaccurate impression of a particular course or instructor from reading forum postings.

Another major problem with basing your decisions on student comments is that you know absolutely nothing about the individual students who post their opinions. These students may be completely different from you, with different strengths and weaknesses, and they might learn best in different formats. The bottom line is that you just don't know.

When you find historical grade distributions, you see hard evidence demonstrating how the instructor has actually graded. By looking at past performance, you put yourself in a good position to determine how she may grade in the future. That's a stark contrast with relying on the musings of one or more previous students whom you know nothing about.

If, however, you are unable to obtain any grade distribution histories for a course you want to take, or a similar course taught by the same instructor, it will usually make sense to take a quick look at comments made by other students about particular instructors. Some information is probably better than none at all. But, given the uncertainties surrounding subjective information, give very little weight to it when you select your instructor for a particular course.[30]

5. **If you learn that a significant percentage of students withdrew from a course during a previous semester, you should usually assume that those students withdrew rather than earn a failing grade.**

On some websites that show the distribution of grades for an instructor's course, you can see not only the final grades of the students who finished the course, but the percentage of students who withdrew from the course prior to the end of the semester and received no grade. When this information is available, you should include it in your analysis.

Some students withdraw from courses for personal reasons that have nothing to do with their performance. In other instances, though, students receive permission from the instructor or the university to withdraw from a course when they are on track to earn a failing grade.

You probably won't be able to learn why students withdrew from a course. But anytime you learn that a significant percentage of students did so, it should raise a red flag. Unless you know otherwise, assume that those students withdrew for grade- and performance-related reasons. Then, when you consider the distribution of final grades, assume that the percentage of low course grades should have been higher.

Questions to Ask Yourself Each Time You Professor Shop

As you can see, you need to think critically whenever you professor shop. Each time you begin to professor shop, ask yourself the following questions:

- Has the instructor taught the identical course before?

- If the instructor hasn't taught this exact course, has she taught a course with a similar format geared to similarly situated students?

- Is there anything about the past courses that are different from the course available to you that could make the past grade distribution a poor predictor of the way the instructor will grade your course? Ensure that you have a reason to believe the grade distribution of the course you want to take will be similar.

- Can you find out the number or percentage of students who withdrew from this course during previous semesters? To the extent that you can, unless you know otherwise, assume that those students would have earned a poor grade had they completed the course.

- How does the percentage of As, Bs, Cs, Ds, and Fs a particular instructor awarded compare with the grade distribution of other instructors teaching the same course, or another one available to you that fulfills the same degree requirement?

By asking yourself these questions, you can make more informed decisions.

Applying the GPAMaxx Strategy on Your Own

At this point, we shift gears. The first six parts of this book provided you with background information to help you approach college strategically. In Part VII, we show you how to apply what you have learned and use the GPAMaxx Strategy to position yourself for success. You learn here how to develop your own university game plan with the GPAMaxx Game Plan Module. You also learn how to select well-suited and GPA-friendly courses with the GPAMaxx Course Selection Module.

By applying what you learn here, you can set the stage for an on-time college graduation (and maybe even an early one) and for getting high grades that can help open the door to a bright future.

CHAPTER

16

Developing Your University Game Plan with the GPAMaxx Strategy

This Chapter Covers

- A step-by-step guide to developing your university game plan using the GPAMaxx Game Plan Module

One of the two primary objectives of the GPAMaxx Strategy is to ensure that you graduate on time or early. To help you meet that objective, we developed the first part of the GPAMaxx Strategy, the GPAMaxx Game Plan Module. This is a step-by-step approach that will help you develop your own university game plan to complete the course requirements for your degree efficiently, and, often, more cost-effectively.

In this chapter, we show you how to develop your university game plan by working your way through a series of steps, a number of which require you to chart out information related to your degree requirements. Going through all the steps takes several hours, but the process will ultimately save you a lot of time.

Why You Need a University Game Plan

Too many college students never take the time to develop a general university completion game plan that helps them do two things:

- Understand the course requirements they need to complete to progress toward graduation

- Uncover the different options they have to fulfill their required coursework

Because they don't do so, students often make strategic errors that include the following:

- Taking courses they aren't required to take and that don't apply toward their degree

- Neglecting to take courses they need, at the time they should take them

- Taking courses at their university for which they could have earned credit by examination

- Taking courses in their weakest subjects at their university instead of taking an equivalent course for transfer credit at a different college where the grade earned would not affect their institutional GPA

- Taking a course to satisfy a requirement when an alternate course would have been more suitable for them

These strategic blunders can have serious consequences. They not only can prevent students from graduating on time and cause them to spend money unnecessarily, but can hurt their GPAs as well. A lower GPA can in turn narrow the range of employment, graduate school, and other opportunities open to these students after they graduate.

Developing a university game plan with the GPAMaxx Game Plan Module helps minimize these risks. You develop a game plan to complete your course requirements on time. You analyze each

A University Game Plan and Your Major (or Lack of One)

Give serious thought to what you might want to major in before you arrive at your university. The course requirements you must complete during your first year at college can be very different depending on your major. Especially in majors that have a lot of sequential coursework—such as STEM (science, technology, engineering, and math) subjects—you can easily fall off track to graduate on time by failing to take certain courses during your first semester.

If you haven't yet decided on a major but have narrowed your choices down to a couple of potential ones, obtain a copy of the degree plan for each of those majors. Your initial game plan should include courses that satisfy the course requirements for all your potential majors. For example, if you're not sure whether you want to major in anthropology or business administration, each of which has a mathematics distribution requirement, you want to make sure that any math course you complete fulfills the math requirement for both majors.

But what if you have no clear idea of what you will choose as your major? Find out whether your university has a generic degree plan for undecided majors that sets forth the basic general education requirements. If one isn't available, you should be able to find the general education requirements and the courses that will fulfill them on your university's website or in its catalog. If they're difficult to find, call or email the registrar and ask for a copy.

By thinking about your major now, you can save a lot of time—not to mention frustration—later.

degree requirement, learning the different course options you have to fulfill it. This helps you avoid the mistakes many students make. Because you analyze your degree requirements, you won't unwittingly take any courses that don't satisfy requirements, and you won't waste your time and money taking courses for which you can earn CBE instead. You also determine whether taking the course at a different college for transfer credit would be a better option. You make sure you complete courses that serve as prerequisites for other courses on schedule; this keeps you from falling off track to graduate on time. Doing these things helps you complete college efficiently and, often, more cost-effectively.

There's a catch, though. Creating your own university game plan requires you to do your homework. You'll have to find and record information, keep it at your fingertips, and periodically update and revise your master plan. Unless you put your game plan in writing, it's highly unlikely you will recall many of your findings a semester or a year later. Without a written record of the information you have already gathered, you're almost certain to make strategic errors in executing your overall plan, selecting individual courses, and satisfying requirements.

Graduating Early and a University Game Plan

A number of you may want to graduate not just on time, but early. If you are one of these students, developing a detailed game plan is an absolute necessity. Say you wish to graduate two semesters early. You will need to complete at least 30 credit hours, or 10 three-credit-hour courses and the equivalent of two semesters of coursework, early.

But there's more to graduating early than just racking up the required number of credit hours. You will also have to be meticulous about how you fill out your academic calendar each semester. Many majors are designed around building blocks of courses; you can't take some courses until you complete certain other courses that serve as prerequisites. To graduate early, you must find ways to fulfill all your prerequisites ahead of schedule. For many students, this—not a lack of sufficient credit hours—proves to be the biggest obstacle to graduating early.

The GPAMaxx Game Plan Module can help you develop a game plan to graduate early. Maximizing your use of credit by examination is one step in this game plan, allowing you to skip certain courses entirely and saving you valuable time. In another game plan step, you develop a potential action plan to fulfill requirements by taking courses for transfer credit at other colleges. This lets you learn which courses you can take for transfer credit at other colleges, not to mention where and when you can do this. Using the GPAMaxx Game Plan Module also forces you to understand your course requirements much more thoroughly. You can then better ensure you complete all your prerequisite courses ahead of schedule and position yourself to graduate early.

Graduating early takes careful planning, but the rewards can be huge. If the possibility interests you, invest the time you need to develop a detailed game plan that charts your road to graduating early. You may be very glad you did.

Who Was the GPAMaxx Game Plan Module Designed For?

We've tailored the GPAMaxx Game Plan Module used in this chapter to students who have yet to begin college or only recently started. We focus primarily on showing you how to develop your own game plan to satisfy general education and other introductory course requirements, rather than advanced coursework in your major. A couple of the suggested steps shown here may be of less help to students who have already completed their general education and other introductory requirements.

Why is this? Once you complete your general education and other introductory course requirements, you may not have as many options as you might like to fulfill a particular requirement. Earning credit by examination is often not an option in higher-level courses. Further, in many instances, a university will require students to take most of the higher-level courses in their major on campus, not at other colleges for transfer credit.

If you've already completed your general education and other introductory course requirements, you should still work your way through the steps of the GPAMaxx Game Plan Module. But do so with the understanding that you may be able to skip some steps altogether.

Using the GPAMaxx Game Plan Module: A Primer

The GPAMaxx Game Plan Module includes tables you can use as a model for gathering the information you need to develop your own game plan. You can also download them from our website, www.GPAMaxx.com. Because every student is unique, feel free to adjust the tables to better fit your own situation.

To create the most useful game plan that you can, be sure to work your way through all the steps, do all the related exercises, and keep all the information you generate in one place. You want to have a detailed record of what you uncover so that you can refer to it later.

The diagram on the next page provides an overview of what the GPAMaxx Game Plan Module looks like. Immediately following that, we'll walk through each of its nine steps individually to show you how to develop your own game plan.

GPAMaxx Game Plan Module*
(Incoming/Early Stage Student Module)

STEP 1 — Find out your university's requirements to graduate with academic honors

STEP 2 — Get and review a copy of your degree plan

STEP 3 — Familiarize yourself with the rules and policies relating to the completion of your degree

STEP 4 — Evaluate where you currently stand

STEP 5 — Evaluate what you already know

STEP 6 — Discover strategic alternatives to taking courses at your university

STEP 7 — Create a credit by examination action plan

STEP 8 — Create a transfer course action plan

STEP 9 — Create and update your own ongoing university master game plan

* Download the GPAMaxx Game Plan Module from our website: www.GPAMaxx.com.

STEP 1

Find Out Your University's Requirements to Graduate with Academic Honors

Before you begin to develop your university game plan, you want to know what your university requires to graduate with honors. The goal isn't to simply get your degree, after all, but to thrive academically and be a top student.

Many universities bestow a variety of honors on their top students. These may include GPA-based honors such as magna cum laude, election to prestigious academic honor societies like Phi Beta Kappa, and honors in your major or college. You need to learn the minimum GPA required to graduate with each of these honors; you should also find out if there are any required courses or non-GPA-related requirements for graduating with honors. To be eligible to graduate with honors, for example, most universities require their students to complete a minimum number of credit hours there, not at other colleges.

You can often find these requirements in your university's catalog or on its website. Once you have this information in hand, you can move on to the next step.

STEP 2

Get and Review a Copy of Your Degree Plan

This is an essential component of GPAMaxx Cardinal Rule #1: *Know Your University Road Map—Your Degree Plan.* First, obtain a copy of the degree plan for your major so that you can see all the course requirements you must fulfill in order to graduate. Then review your degree plan to get a basic understanding of the requirements you must fulfill early in your college career. You don't want to take courses that won't count toward your degree.

STEP 3

Familiarize Yourself with the Rules and Policies Relating to the Completion of Your Degree

You need more than just a copy of your degree plan. You also need to understand your university's rules and policies regarding the ways you may satisfy the course requirements for your degree.

Although this is by no means an exhaustive list, here are some questions for which you should obtain answers:

- How many credit hours are required in order to graduate?

- How many credit hours must you complete in residence at your university?

- How many credit hours in your major and minor must you complete in residence?

- Does your university allow you to take pass/fail courses? If so, what are the policies relating to the use of such courses, including the maximum number you can apply toward your degree?

- What are the general policies of your university regarding the use of credit by examination, including:

  - Does your university allow you to earn CBE throughout your studies, or are you allowed to do so only before you accumulate a certain number of credit hours?

  - How many credit hours in total will your university permit you to fulfill through CBE?

  - For which courses is your university willing to award CBE, and through which exams? What are the minimum scores you need on each exam to earn CBE?

- In what instances does your university not award credit hours for exams for CBE, but instead offer only an exemption from taking a particular course or placement into a higher-level course?

- What are the general policies of your university regarding the use of transfer coursework, including:

  - Do you need to obtain permission from your university to take courses for transfer credit at other colleges? If so, what are the procedures to get permission?

  - What (if any) introductory or general education courses must you take in residence at your university?

  - When you take courses for transfer credit at other colleges, does your university average the grades into your institutional GPA? If so, in what instances?

- What are the restrictions on online coursework at your university?

- If you think you may want to study abroad at any point during your studies, what are the options available to students in your major at your university? Find out if your university includes the grades from study abroad courses in its institutional GPA calculation. Careful planning is essential for most semester- or year-long study abroad experiences. Start early.

Don't expect these rules, policies, and the related information to be easy to locate or clearly explained. Where you find this information varies from university to university, and you'll probably have to hunt around for at least some of it. Your university won't likely deliver all the information you need in one handy packet.

Begin by looking in your university's undergraduate catalog. Then search its website for anything you haven't been able to locate. If you don't find the remaining information you need there, email your questions to the admissions or registrar's office. Even if staff members don't respond with answers, they should at least tell you where to find them or who to contact for further assistance.

Once you familiarize yourself with the requirements of your degree as well as any restrictions and limitations, you can begin to analyze those requirements.

Special Considerations for Students at Two-Year Colleges

The degree requirements that matter most are the ones for the university where you plan to complete your bachelor's degree. If you hope to earn an associate's degree or study at a two-year college before you enroll at a four-year university, find out how your courses at the two-year college will be recognized by the university you plan to attend afterward.

Under the rules in effect in some states, earning an associate's degree means you automatically satisfy all the general education course requirements needed to complete your bachelor's degree at any public university in that state. Because these rules vary considerably among different states and universities, check with both the two-year college you attend and the university to which you hope to transfer.

STEP 4

Evaluate Where You Currently Stand

Even before you start college, you may be on your way to fulfilling some course requirements toward your degree. For example, if you are taking or have taken AP or IB courses in high school, your score on the national exam may qualify you to earn CBE. If you are taking or have taken dual-enrollment courses, you may be able to earn high school credit and university-level credit hours simultaneously. You need to evaluate where you stand.

Review the course and distribution requirements under your degree plan and ask yourself the following questions:

- Are you working to satisfy, or have you already satisfied, any course or distribution requirements through CBE?

- If you are scheduled to take, or have already taken, AP, IB, or other exams offered by national testing programs, learn whether your university awards CBE based on the results. If so, find out the requirements those exams can fulfill, as well as the minimum score you must obtain on each to earn CBE.

- Are you taking, or have you already taken, any courses at a college for university-level credit?

- If you take or have already taken any courses for which you earned credit hours at any colleges, including dual-enrollment classes at your high school, find out whether those hours transfer to your intended university. If they do, find out exactly which degree requirements they fulfill.

Once you answer these questions, document in writing the requirements you have already satisfied or expect to fulfill, exactly how you meet them, and the things you need to do to make sure you receive credit hours toward your degree for them.

Create a table like Table 16–1 to keep track of this information.

Table 16-1

STEP 4*
Evaluate Where You Currently Stand

Name of Exam for CBE/College-Level Course Already Taken or Taking	Name and Number of Equivalent Course at Your University	Degree Plan Requirement (Distribution/Major/Other)	Degree Plan Requirement Already Completed/When to Complete? (Semester/Year)	Steps to Get Credit at Your University

* Download this table from our website: www.GPAMaxx.com.

—————————————— STEP 5 ——————————————

Evaluate What You Already Know

You probably know quite a bit about some of the subjects that make up the course requirements under your degree plan. Many general education courses are identical or closely related to subjects you studied in high school. If you're like most students, though, you won't give much thought to how you can leverage what you already know to fulfill degree plan requirements.

In some subjects, your high school knowledge may suffice for you to earn CBE with only a little additional studying. And we aren't just talking about what you learn in honors, AP, or IB classes, either. The knowledge you acquire even in regular high school courses may make it feasible for you—especially with additional review—to earn CBE for the equivalent courses at your university. For example, if you took psychology in high school, you may only need a little additional review to score high enough on the CLEP Introductory Psychology exam to earn CBE for the equivalent university course.

In addition, don't discount the value of knowledge and skills you acquired outside the classroom. You may be surprised at how much you already know. For instance, if you're a native or fluent speaker in any language other than English, your university may grant you CBE for your language fluency that fulfills your foreign language requirement, or earns you elective credit hours toward your degree.

Countless students overlook their existing skill sets in many subjects, neglecting to leverage them when they pursue their undergraduate degrees. It's your job to make sure you assess your own base of knowledge and determine how you can use it to satisfy course requirements for your degree. No one is going to do it for you.

Create a table like Table 16–2 to keep track of this information.

Table 16-2

STEP 5*
Evaluate What You Already Know

Name of Course in High School / Skill or Knowledge	Name and Number of Equivalent University Course	Degree Plan Requirement (Distribution/Major/Other)

STEP 6

Discover Strategic Alternatives to Taking Courses at Your University

There are often ways to fulfill course requirements aside from taking the courses in residence at your university. Two main ways are through credit by examination and transfer coursework. Although some students fulfill numerous degree requirements through them, the vast majority never explore these options in the depth that they should. For you to maximize the advantages that these alternatives can offer you, you need to discover the full extent to which they are available to you.

For each degree plan requirement, determine whether your university requires you to complete a course on campus. If it does, you have no choice: you must take that course at your university.

If you don't have to take a course in residence, learn what other strategic alternatives you have to satisfy the degree requirement— namely, whether you can take an exam to earn CBE or take an equivalent course at a different college for transfer credit.

As you learn your alternatives, create a table like Table 16–3 to keep track of this information. That way, you can refer to the information when you need it.

Table 16-3

STEP 6*
Discover Strategic Alternatives to Taking Courses at Your University

Degree Plan Requirement (Distribution/Major/Other)	Name and Number of Each Course That Satisfies Requirement	Required to Be Taken in Residence at Your University? (Yes/No)	Possible to Earn CBE Instead? List Exams and Minimum Score	Transfer Course Equivalents at Local Colleges

---

STEP 7

Create a Credit by Examination Action Plan

After you complete the exercises in Steps 1 through 6, you have at your fingertips the information you need to develop your own action plan to fulfill course requirements through CBE. As you worked through the previous steps, you probably discovered that you can use CBE to fulfill many of these requirements. Now it's time to develop your own action plan that outlines the requirements you will try to satisfy through CBE, and in what order you will take the exams.

To create an effective CBE action plan, you'll need the following:

- A copy of your degree plan (Step 2)

- Access to your university's policies relating to CBE (Step 3)

- The completed table listing the course distribution requirements you have already satisfied (Step 4)

- The completed table of course requirements in subjects you already know something about (Step 5)

- The completed table of course requirements you can satisfy through CBE and transfer courses (Step 6)

You will also want to refer to "Prioritizing Your Use of Credit by Examination" in Chapter 10. That section can help you decide the order in which you want to take exams to earn CBE.

Now that you've assembled all this information in a single place, you're ready to develop your own CBE action plan that sets forth how you hope to use CBE to fulfill your course requirements. Put your CBE action plan into writing by creating a table like Table 16–4.

Table 16-4

STEP 7*
Create a Credit by Examination Action Plan

Priority for Study (#)	Name and Type of Exam to Earn CBE	Minimum Score Required to Earn CBE	Name and Number of Equivalent Course at Your University	Degree Plan Requirement (Distribution/Major/ Other)	Deadline to Satisfy Requirement at Your University

---
STEP 8

Create a Transfer Course Action Plan

Once you develop your CBE action plan, consider how you can use transfer courses to satisfy degree requirements that would involve courses you expect to be difficult, harshly graded, or otherwise problematic if you were to take them at your university. It often makes sense to take such courses at a different college where the grades you earn in those courses won't affect your institutional GPA or where those courses may be easier for whatever reason.

CBE is generally preferable to transfer coursework as a way to fulfill the general education and introductory course requirements of your degree plan, but you still need a strategy for using transfer coursework to fulfill especially difficult and otherwise problematic courses.

Why? There are two key reasons.

First, in some cases, your university may not allow you to earn CBE for a course that satisfies a particular requirement under your degree plan. Your only strategic alternative to taking the course at your university may be to take it for transfer credit at a different college.

Second, you may not score high enough on the exam to earn CBE for some courses. If you don't earn CBE for requirements in your weaker subjects or other GPA-risky courses, it can make sense to take them for transfer credit at a different college.

Put your transfer course action plan into writing by creating a table like Table 16–5.

Table 16-5

STEP 8*
Create a Transfer Course Action Plan

Name and Number of Course at Your University	Degree Plan Requirement (Distribution/ Major/Other)	Equivalent Transfer Course and Name of College Where Offered	Can You Earn CBE for This Requirement Rather Than Taking Transfer Course? (Yes/No)	When Is Equivalent Transfer Course Offered?	Feasible for You to Enroll in Transfer Course? (Yes/No)

STEP 9

Create and Update Your Own Ongoing University Master Game Plan

Now that you've completed the first eight steps, it's time to pull all this information together to create a university master game plan that specifies how and when you hope to complete each degree requirement. Create a table like Table 16–6 that summarizes the information you have already organized.

This table shouldn't be overly complicated. Leave the details in the tables you previously created, but keep them with your master game plan so you can easily refer to them if needed.

This is the most important step, so spend as much time as you need. Without a master game plan that clearly spells things out, it's all too easy to make poor decisions that can delay your graduation and make you miss opportunities to both protect and raise your GPA through well-chosen courses.

As you progress through college, you will need to maintain and regularly update your master game plan. By doing this, you can stay on top of your degree requirements and the options you have to fulfill them.

Table 16-6

STEP 9*
Create and Update Your Own Ongoing University Master Game Plan

Degree Plan Requirement (Distribution/Major/Other)	Name and Number of Each Course That Satisfies Requirement	How You Hope to Satisfy Requirement (On Campus/CBE/Transfer Course/Other)	Specific Exams to Earn CBE or Transfer Courses to Earn Credit	Requirement Already Completed? When to Complete? (Semester/Year)

* Download this table from our website: www.GPAMaxx.com.

You and Your University Game Plan: An Ongoing Relationship

Now that you've reviewed the nine steps, make time in your schedule to obtain the information you need, and complete each step. Pulling everything together will require some effort, but it will be energy well spent.

Your university game plan is a document that you'll review and revise frequently throughout college. When you first create it, you won't be looking into the future to plan your entire university career. If you're still in high school or just starting college, you'll probably change your mind about many things over time—your major, the courses you want to take, and perhaps even the university from which you plan to graduate. It would be impractical and unrealistic to attempt to plan your courses for all of college in an afternoon and expect to have everything set in stone.

For now, you only need to develop a preliminary plan for the way you expect to fulfill the general education and other introductory course requirements under your degree plan. As you progress through your studies, expect to modify and update your game plan whenever your circumstances and the type of coursework you take change. You can expect a major transition, for example, when you move from taking predominantly general education courses to taking primarily courses in your major and minor.

If you always remember to research your options for fulfilling degree plan requirements, you'll be comfortable updating and adjusting your university game plan whenever necessary.

Selecting Your Courses with the GPAMaxx Strategy

This Chapter Covers

- A step-by-step guide to selecting your courses using the GPAMaxx Course Selection Module

---

In Chapter 16, you learned about the first part of the GPAMaxx Strategy, the GPAMaxx Game Plan Module. It addresses one of the two primary objectives of the GPAMaxx Strategy, graduating on time or early. In this chapter, we tackle the second primary objective: maximizing your college GPA. To help you meet that objective, we developed the second part of the GPAMaxx Strategy, the GPAMaxx Course Selection Module. This is a step-by-step approach that helps you select your courses each semester. Following this seven-stage module will help you find well-fitting courses and fulfill your degree requirements efficiently.

It's impossible to overstate the importance of strategically selecting the right courses. When you take courses that are a poor fit for you, it's often difficult to get the high grades you want in them—no matter how hard you study. Ill-suited courses can have a real negative impact on your GPA.

In contrast, when you select courses that interest you, play to your strengths, and are taught in your preferred format by an instructor who grades students favorably, you set the stage for success.

Therefore, it's essential to try to find those kinds of courses every semester. At the same time, you want to take only courses that count toward your degree and to fulfill your requirements efficiently. You don't want to waste valuable time and tuition dollars on courses you don't need to take.

The GPAMaxx Course Selection Module can help you do this. Using it lets you more fully comprehend all the choices you have to complete your degree requirements. This helps you select good-fitting courses and make better, more informed decisions about how to fulfill those requirements.

Using the GPAMaxx Course Selection Module: A Primer

The GPAMaxx Course Selection Module uses a seven-stage process to help you select your courses. Since multiple courses often fulfill a degree plan requirement, you initially focus on a degree plan requirement rather than an individual course. You start by gathering information about the courses and other options (such as credit by examination) that fulfill each requirement. Then you analyze all your choices, weigh all the considerations, and select the course that seems the best fit for you.

Keep in mind that the GPAMaxx Course Selection Module is a tool to help pick your college courses each semester before you register. If you have yet to begin college, you won't use this module until you select your first-semester courses. Before then, you'll want to focus more on developing your university game plan with the GPAMaxx Game Plan Module. If you're already in college, however, the GPAMaxx Course Selection Module can help you every time you choose your courses for an upcoming semester.

When using the GPAMaxx Course Selection Module, be sure to work your way through each stage, do all the related exercises, and keep all the information you generate in one place. You want to have a detailed record of your choices when you register for courses.

The diagram below provides an overview of the seven stages of the GPAMaxx Course Selection Module. In the pages that follow, we'll walk you through each of the seven stages individually. For each stage, we provide a view of its steps in a flow chart and then describe each step. By doing so, we hope to provide you with an even clearer understanding of what you should be doing at each stage as you analyze your courses.

GPAMaxx Course Selection Module*

STAGE I	Choose a degree plan requirement and discover which courses fulfill it
STAGE II	Discover your credit by examination (CBE) options
STAGE III	Discover your transfer course options
STAGE IV	Investigate your potential courses
STAGE V	Go professor shopping
STAGE VI	Weigh your options to fulfill your degree plan requirement
STAGE VII	Decide how to fulfill your degree plan requirement

* Download the GPAMaxx Course Selection Module charts from our website: www.GPAMaxx.com.

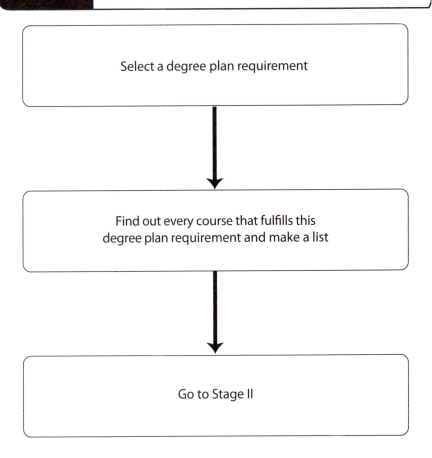

STAGE I Choose a Degree Plan Requirement and Discover Which Courses Fulfill It

Select a degree plan requirement

Find out every course that fulfills this degree plan requirement and make a list

Go to Stage II

STAGE I

Choose a Degree Plan Requirement and Discover Which Courses Fulfill It

Step 1.   Select a degree plan requirement.

Every course you take should satisfy a requirement toward your degree. Begin your analysis of potential courses by selecting a degree plan requirement you need to fulfill. Focus first on the requirement rather than on any individual course.

Step 2.   Find every course that fulfills this degree plan requirement and make a list.

Even if you think you already know the specific course you want to take and which instructor you prefer, make a list of every course that fulfills this degree plan requirement. Don't limit your list to courses that interest you or to ones you already know about. Making a comprehensive list eliminates the risk of overlooking courses that might be a good fit for you.

Making a list can be helpful for another reason: there's a good chance you won't be able to register for your first-choice course, especially if you're a freshman or sophomore. After seniors and juniors have registered, your first-choice course may not have space, or at least not in the section taught by your first-choice instructor. You need to be prepared with a second choice (and possibly even a third choice) if your first choice is unavailable.

Step 3.   After you make a comprehensive list, go to Stage II.

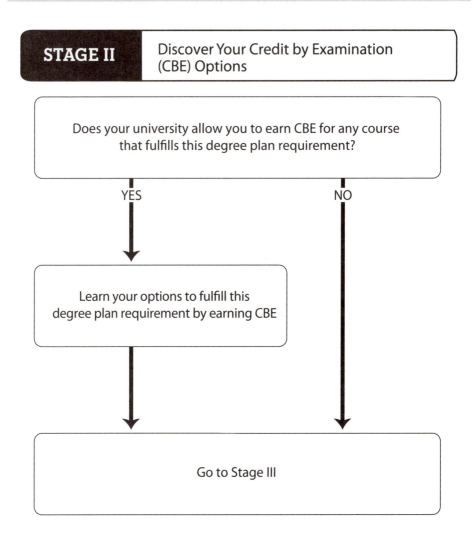

STAGE II   Discover Your Credit by Examination (CBE) Options

Does your university allow you to earn CBE for any course that fulfills this degree plan requirement?

YES   NO

Learn your options to fulfill this degree plan requirement by earning CBE

Go to Stage III

STAGE II

Discover Your Credit by Examination (CBE) Options

CBE can be a terrific way to fulfill degree plan requirements without taking a course at all. As you consider your options, keep in mind what you learned in Chapter 9, Credit by Examination: An Overview, and Chapter 10, Making the Most of Credit by Examination.

Step 1.   **Does your university allow you to earn CBE for any course that fulfills this degree plan requirement?**

- If YES, go to Step 2.

- If NO, go directly to Stage III.

Step 2.   **Learn your options to fulfill this degree plan requirement by earning CBE.**

Find out which exams you can take to earn CBE for each course that fulfills this degree requirement. So you don't overlook this information later, be sure to note for each exam:

- The type of exam (for example, CLEP or DSST)

- The minimum score required to earn CBE

- When and where the exam is offered

If you've already developed your university game plan using the GPAMaxx Game Plan Module, you should have compiled this information.

Step 3.   **Once you have noted all of this information, go to Stage III.**

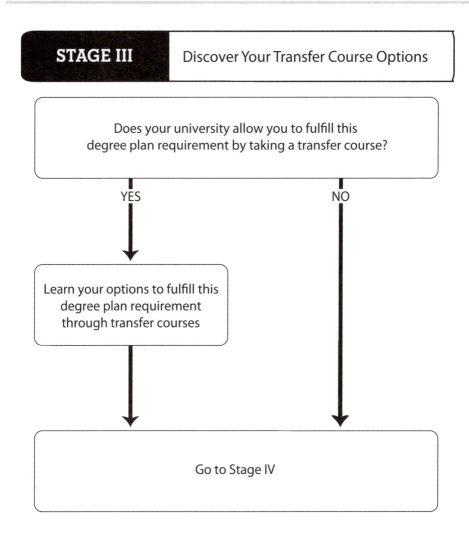

STAGE III   Discover Your Transfer Course Options

Does your university allow you to fulfill this degree plan requirement by taking a transfer course?

YES

NO

Learn your options to fulfill this degree plan requirement through transfer courses

Go to Stage IV

STAGE III

Discover Your Transfer Course Options

In certain situations, it can make sense to fulfill degree plan requirements by taking courses for transfer credit at colleges other than your own. As you consider your transfer course options, keep in mind what you learned in Chapter 11, Taking Transfer Courses: An Overview.

Step 1.   **Does your university allow you to fulfill this degree plan requirement by taking a transfer course?**

- If YES, go to Step 2.

- If NO, go directly to Stage IV.

Step 2.   **Learn your options to fulfill this degree plan requirement through transfer courses.**

For each course that fulfills this degree plan requirement, find out about the transfer course equivalents at other colleges. You should consider transfer courses only at colleges where it makes sense for you to attend classes. So that you don't overlook this information later, be sure to note:

- The equivalent course name and the college that offers it

- When each college usually offers the equivalent course

If you've already developed your university game plan using the GPAMaxx Game Plan Module, you should have compiled this information.

Step 3.   **Once you have noted all of this information, go to Stage IV.**

STAGE IV Investigate Your Potential Courses

For every course that fulfills this degree plan requirement:

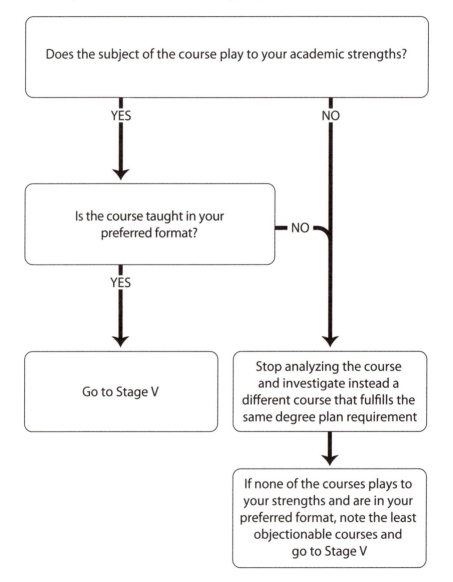

Does the subject of the course play to your academic strengths?

YES — Is the course taught in your preferred format? — YES — Go to Stage V

NO — Stop analyzing the course and investigate instead a different course that fulfills the same degree plan requirement

If none of the courses plays to your strengths and are in your preferred format, note the least objectionable courses and go to Stage V

STAGE IV

Investigate Your Potential Courses

Whenever possible, you want to take courses that play to your strengths and are in your preferred format. To minimize the risk of choosing a poorly fitting course, you need to analyze each potential course to find out if seems right for you. Keep in mind GPAMaxx Cardinal Rule #2: *Know Yourself as a Student*, and what you learned in Part V, Getting to Know Yourself.

Follow the steps below for every course that fulfills the degree plan requirement you are investigating:

Step 1. **Does the subject of the course play to your academic strengths?**

- If YES, go to Step 2.

- If NO, stop analyzing this course. Instead, start analyzing a different course that fulfills the same degree plan requirement.

Step 2. **Is the course taught in your preferred format? If a course isn't in, or reasonably close to, your ideal instructional format and your ideal grading format, the answer is no.**

- If YES, go to Stage V.

- If NO, stop analyzing this course. Instead, start investigating a different course that fulfills the same degree plan requirement.

Step 3. **If none of the courses plays to your strengths and is in your preferred format, note the least objectionable courses and go to Stage V.**

For some of your degree plan requirements, there may not be any single course that's a good fit, or even a decent fit, for you. In these cases, you need to know your "least bad" options. These are the courses you will investigate further.

STAGE V   Go Professor Shopping

For every course that you decided to analyze further after Step IV:

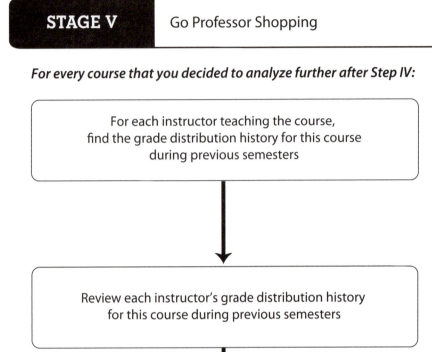

For each instructor teaching the course,
find the grade distribution history for this course
during previous semesters

Review each instructor's grade distribution history
for this course during previous semesters

Go to Stage VI

STAGE V

Go Professor Shopping

You want to professor shop to learn how each instructor typically grades students in the courses you are considering. Keep in mind GPAMaxx Cardinal Rule #3: *Know How to Professor Shop*, and what you learned in Part VI, Learning to Professor Shop.

Follow the steps below for every course that you decided to analyze further after completing Stage IV:

Step 1. **For each instructor teaching this course, find his or her grade distribution history for this course during previous semesters.**

Try to locate each instructor's grade distribution histories for this course. You want to find out exactly how he or she graded students in this class during previous semesters.

If you are unable to obtain breakdowns of the grades each instructor awarded, look for other information about the instructor.

Step 2. **Review and take detailed notes about each instructor's grade distribution history for this course during previous semesters.**

For each instructor, write down what percentage of his or her class received As, Bs, and so on during previous semesters. If multiple instructors teach the same course, determine which ones generally award higher grades in the course. Even if you can't find out exactly how instructors graded students during previous semesters, try to get a sense of what type of graders they are. For more on the different types of graders, refer to Chapter 5, Making the Grade: What You Should Know About University Grading Practices.

Step 3. **Once you have noted this information, go to Stage VI.**

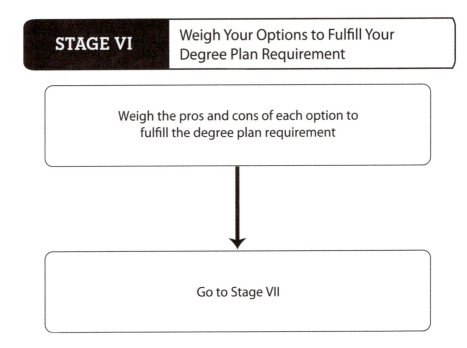

STAGE VI   Weigh Your Options to Fulfill Your Degree Plan Requirement

Weigh the pros and cons of each option to fulfill the degree plan requirement

Go to Stage VII

STAGE VI

Weigh Your Options to Fulfill
Your Degree Plan Requirement

You've spent the first five stages of this module gathering a lot of information. Just by collecting the information and learning about each of your options, you may already know how you hope to fulfill the degree plan requirement.

Even if you're pretty sure you know your choice, you should evaluate all the information you've compiled to be sure you haven't overlooked any options. Begin Stage VI only after you go through Stages I through V with every course that fulfills this degree plan requirement.

Step 1.   **Weigh the pros and cons of each option to fulfill the degree plan requirement.**

Evaluating the ways to fulfill a degree plan requirement is often challenging. You need to think strategically. As you consider how you will fulfill the degree plan requirement, consider each of the following options to the extent that it is available to you:

- *Earning Credit by Examination (CBE)*

When you have the option to earn credit hours for a course and have adequate time to prepare for the exam, trying to earn CBE is usually a no-lose situation. If you don't score high enough to earn CBE, it won't hurt your GPA. And if your score is high enough, even just barely, you'll not only earn credit hours toward your degree, but you'll likely save time and money as well.

An exception to this advice might be when a course serves as a foundation for higher-level courses that you plan to take later in your college career. If you lack a solid base of knowledge in the subject and use CBE to bypass an entry-level course, you run the risk of being unprepared for higher-level courses. Consider your use of CBE carefully in this situation.

For more on CBE, refer to Chapter 9, Credit by Examination: An Overview, and Chapter 10, Making the Most of Credit by Examination.

- *Taking a Transfer Course*

Completing a course for transfer credit at a different college makes sense when you have a strategic reason to do so. A majority of public universities don't include grades from transfer courses in the institutional GPA. If that's the case at your university, and you expect a particular course to be especially risky to your institutional GPA, you can protect yourself by taking the course for transfer credit at a different college. You'll earn credit for the course, but without a grade that could lower your institutional GPA.

On the flip side, if you think you will get a good grade in a particular course, take it at your own university so that the grade gets averaged into your institutional GPA.

For more information about taking courses for transfer credit, refer to Chapter 11, Taking Transfer Courses: An Overview.

- *Taking a Course at Your University*

When multiple courses at your university fulfill the same degree plan requirement, you want to compare them all and find the one that offers you the best chances of doing well.

This may sound easy, but it's often not. You may not find a course that interests you, plays to your strengths, is offered in your preferred format, and is taught by an instructor who grades favorably. Many courses you evaluate will likely be less than ideal in one way or another. Maybe the instructor with the most grade-friendly history doesn't teach the course in your preferred format. Or perhaps a course whose topic plays to your strengths is graded on harsh curve.

In situations where it's not clear-cut which course you prefer, you'll need to weigh your potential courses against one another to make an informed decision. As you analyze each course, consider its format, whether it plays to your strengths, and the instructor's grading history. For more on these factors, refer to Part V, Getting to Know Yourself, and Part VI, Learning to Professor Shop.

Step 2.   **Write down your observations and go to Stage VII.**

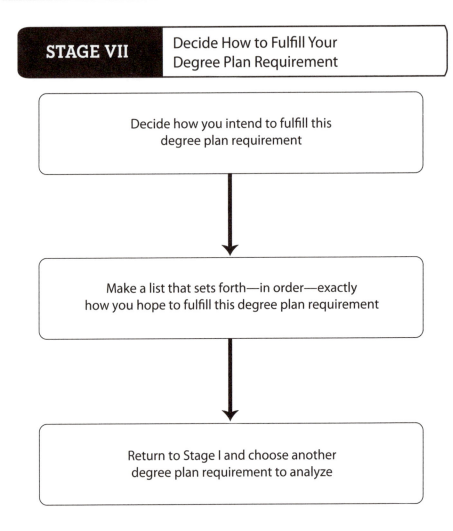

STAGE VII — Decide How to Fulfill Your Degree Plan Requirement

Decide how you intend to fulfill this degree plan requirement

Make a list that sets forth—in order—exactly how you hope to fulfill this degree plan requirement

Return to Stage I and choose another degree plan requirement to analyze

STAGE VII

Decide How to to Fulfill
Your Degree Plan Requirement

In the previous stage, you evaluated the information you compiled. Now it's decision time.

Step 1.   Decide how you intend to fulfill this degree plan requirement.

Once you decide, keep the following in mind:

- If you decide to try to earn CBE, you still need a backup plan in case you don't score high enough on the exam. You must know exactly how you intend to fulfill the requirement in case your exam score doesn't qualify you for CBE.

- If you decide to fulfill a requirement by taking a transfer course instead of an on-campus course, make sure you know exactly when and where you will take it. You want to eliminate any risk that this course could throw you off schedule to fulfill your degree plan requirements.

- For each course you opt to take at your university, don't forget to select a second and possibly a third choice in case there isn't room in your first choice when you register.

Step 2.   Make a list that sets forth—in order—exactly how you hope to fulfill this degree plan requirement.

Write down your choices to fulfill the degree plan requirement in question. List them in order of preference. That way, you can easily remember your preferences for completing this requirement.

Here's an example of what such a list might look like for a student deciding how to fulfill her degree plan's one-course Social Awareness requirement:

	Preference List to Fulfill Social Awareness Degree Plan Requirement
1	Attempt to earn CBE for course Introduction to Sociology with the CLEP exam.
	If unable to score high enough on that exam, then …
2	Attempt to earn CBE for course Introduction to Psychology with the CLEP exam.
	If unable to score high enough on that exam, then …
3	Take Introduction to Sociology with Professor Jones next semester.
	If Professor Jones' section is already full, then …
4	Take Introduction to Sociology with Professor Sweeney.
	If Professor Sweeney's section is already full, then …
5	Take Introduction to Psychology with Professor Watanabe.

Step 3.   Return to Stage I and choose another degree plan requirement to analyze.

Analyzing Your Potential Courses Is Time Well Spent

At this point, you may wonder if using the GPAMaxx Course Selection Module to help you select your courses is a productive use of your time. After all, it takes a while to review all your options to fulfill each degree plan requirement and to find the courses that are likely to be a good fit.

Our answer is an unequivocal yes. Using the GPAMaxx Course Selection Module is a great investment of your time. The adage "an ounce of prevention is worth a pound of cure" rings true here. By spending a few hours reviewing all your potential courses, you can better find those courses in which you can shine. You also reduce the risk of taking courses that are a bad fit for you or in which you might struggle. Because even a single bad grade can significantly lower your GPA, anything you can do to reduce the risk of making a poor choice is time well spent.

Once you get the hang of analyzing your options to satisfy degree plan requirements, the process becomes easier and faster. To demonstrate how students like you can effectively use the GPAMaxx Course Selection Module to select great-fitting courses, we've included several case studies in the section that follows this chapter.

CASE STUDIES

The GPAMaxx Course Selection Module in Action

Now that you are familiar with the GPAMaxx Course Selection
Module, we turn to practical applications. Each of the case studies
that follow presents different strategic considerations that students
face when they use the GPAMaxx Course Selection Module. By
learning how each of our model students uses the GPAMaxx Course
Selection Module to choose courses, you'll see how to put this
module into practice for yourself.

CASE STUDY #1

Selecting Courses for Your General Education Requirements

Kaitlyn, Savvy Rising Freshman

Kaitlyn graduated from high school last week and will be a freshman at State University this fall. Although she hasn't even started college yet, Kaitlyn has some big goals. She wants to be a strong student and graduate from State University with academic honors, then study overseas on a Fulbright scholarship. After that, Kaitlyn would like to attend an elite law school.

To meet all of these goals, she's clearly going to need great grades, so she's very concerned about picking courses that will help her maximize her GPA. At the same time, she wants to complete her degree requirements efficiently and graduate on time. Kaitlyn intends to take full advantage of the GPAMaxx Course Selection Module to help her analyze her course choices and find the most GPA-friendly and efficient ways to fulfill them. She'll work through all seven stages of the GPAMaxx Course Selection Module to do this.

Stage I: Choose a Degree Plan Requirement and Discover Which Courses Fulfill It

As part of State University's general education curriculum, Kaitlyn must complete a three-credit-hour course to fulfill the Fine Arts distribution requirement by the end of her first semester. She opts to analyze this degree plan requirement first.

She finds out that four courses at State University fulfill the Fine Arts requirement. All are offered in the fall. The four courses are:

- Artistic Foundations, a small freshman seminar with a creative arts focus taught by Professor Vance. The final course grade is based on a midterm exam (25 percent) and a final exam (50 percent), each consisting of multiple-choice questions, and an art project that each student must complete independently (25 percent).

- History of Dance, an auditorium-size lecture course taught by Professor Wilson. The final grade is based on the results of two multiple-choice midterm exams (25 percent each) and a multiple-choice final exam (50 percent).

- History of Rock & Roll, an auditorium-size lecture course taught by Professor Xavier. The final grade is based on the results of two midterm exams consisting of essay questions (25 percent each) and a final exam also composed of essay questions (50 percent).

- History of Western Art, a small lecture course whose enrollment is capped at 20 students to facilitate class discussion. Because of the small class size, Professor Young and Professor Zimmer teach separate sections, both using the same grading and instructional formats. The final grade is based on two term papers (20 percent each), a midterm consisting of essay questions (20 percent), a final exam consisting of essay questions (30 percent), and class participation and attendance (10 percent).

Now that she knows which courses fulfill the Fine Arts requirement, Kaitlyn makes a list of them and can begin gathering information about each one.

Stage II: Discover Your Credit by Examination (CBE) Options

Kaitlyn finds out if she can test out of any of these courses by earning CBE. Upon investigating, she learns that State University permits its students to earn CBE for History of Western Art, but not for any of the other courses. If she takes the DSST Art of the Western World exam and earns the minimum score required by State University, she'll be eligible to receive credit for the course without taking it. She also finds out that a testing center in her area offers DSST exams on a walk-in basis. That means she can take the exam whenever she wants. Kaitlyn writes all this information down so she won't forget it.

Stage III: Discover Your Transfer Course Options

Next Kaitlyn looks to see if she can fulfill this degree plan requirement by taking a course at a college other than State University for transfer credit. However, she immediately realizes that she won't be able to do so. In a few weeks, Kaitlyn will travel to Cambodia, where she'll volunteer at an orphanage for the rest of the summer. Since she won't be around this summer to take a course, Kaitlyn doesn't need to explore her transfer course options at all.

Stage IV: Investigate Your Potential Courses

Now Kaitlyn needs to investigate each course that fulfills the Fine Arts requirement. For each course, she's trying to determine whether its subject plays to her academic strengths and if it is taught in her preferred format. Since she wants to select courses that are a good fit, she plans to initially screen out courses that aren't. If a course doesn't play to her strengths or its format doesn't seem well suited for her, she'd rather seek out an alternate course that appears to be a better fit. She'll only analyze these screened-out courses beyond Stage IV if all of her other choices appear to be an equally bad or worse fit.

The first course she analyzes is Artistic Foundations. This course covers a topic that doesn't play to her strengths. Although Kaitlyn wishes she had a bit of Picasso or Michelangelo in her, she's never had any aptitude in the creative arts. Kaitlyn immediately thinks taking this course—one in which 25 percent of her final grade would be based on an art project—seems very risky. In addition, the other 75 percent of the grade is based on the results of multiple-choice exams. Kaitlyn's never been good at multiple-choice exams. In high school she was always the student who aced every essay but struggled to muster more than a B on multiple-choice tests. Based on her high school experiences, Kaitlyn hopes to avoid courses with multiple-choice exams whenever she can.

Recognizing that the subject of this course and its grading format make it a poor fit, Kaitlyn stops analyzing it and strikes it from her list. She'll analyze the remaining other courses first. If those appear equally unsuitable, she can go back and analyze this one further.

Next she analyzes History of Dance. At first glance, Kaitlyn is excited to see this as a choice. She loves to dance, and history was always a strong subject for her in high school.

However, when Kaitlyn analyzes the course, she quickly spots some problems. First, the entire course grade is based on multiple-choice exams. What's more, Kaitlyn sees a possible negative in its instructional format: it's an auditorium-size lecture course. She's never taken a large lecture course before, so she has no idea how she'll like the format. She fears she'll have trouble focusing in a giant lecture hall. Before taking an auditorium-size course, she wants to sit in on a few to get a feel for them. This course has two strikes against it: the grading format and (possibly) the instructional format. It comes off her list.

Now Kaitlyn examines History of Rock & Roll. She likes history and loves rock and roll. And the course sounds really cool. Although she hasn't started college yet, Kaitlyn already knows that she should never pick a course solely on its name. Older friends warned her that many university courses with cool-sounding names turn out to be the opposite, and that catchy names are sometimes just a professor's tactic to recruit gullible students. Kaitlyn's too savvy to make this mistake.

Upon further examination, Kaitlyn realizes that this course might not be a good fit either. Although the exams will consist of essay questions, it's another auditorium-size lecture course. Kaitlyn therefore decides to defer her evaluation of History of Rock & Roll until she reviews her final course option. If that one seems like a better choice for her, she won't bother looking into History of Rock & Roll any further.

The final course Kaitlyn analyzes is History of Western Art. It's a history course, which definitely plays to her strengths. And she finds the course topic interesting. Kaitlyn also likes the fact that both sections are relatively small, with lots of class discussion. In high school, she liked small classes with lots of discussion and interaction. Based on those experiences, this course therefore seems pretty close to her ideal instructional format.

Yet another plus: the grading format. Essay exams, term papers, and class participation will determine her grade. In high school, she did well in all three. Because college instructors usually grade far more stringently than high school teachers, she'll likely have to work hard to earn an A, but at least she likes how the instructor will determine her grade.

Since the format and topic for both sections of History of Western Art appear to be a good fit, Kaitlyn opts to analyze each one further.

Stage V: Go Professor Shopping

Kaitlyn proceeds to professor shop the two instructors who will teach this course. She wants to determine how each one graded during past semesters. She finds a website that shows exactly how each instructor awarded grades for this course in recent semesters.

Here's the grade breakdown for Professor Young's History of Western Art sections during two recent semesters:

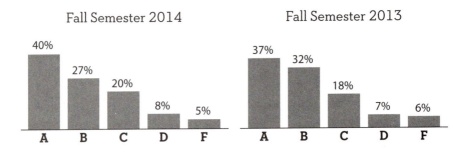

Fall Semester 2014

Fall Semester 2013

And here's the grade breakdown for Professor Zimmer's History of Western Art sections:

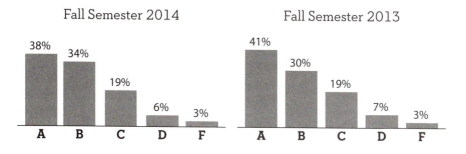

Fall Semester 2014   Fall Semester 2013

Kaitlyn notices that both Professor Young and Professor Zimmer awarded a fairly high percentage of As and Bs in past semesters. She senses that both professors grade favorably and aren't likely to be drill sergeant instructors. Kaitlyn can't tell whether one is an easier grader than the other based on their grading histories, however, so she sees no reason to prefer one over the other.

Stage VI: Weigh Your Options to Fulfill Your Degree Plan Requirement

Now Kaitlyn must weigh all of the options to fulfill her Fine Arts requirement. She must consider whether she should try to earn CBE for History of Western Art or take the course. She must also consider which of the two instructors she prefers.

State University requires its students to fulfill the Fine Arts requirement by the end of their first semester. That means that if Kaitlyn wants to try to earn CBE, she must take the exam before she starts college. She can take the DSST Art of the Western World exam at a nearby testing center on a walk-in basis, but she doesn't have much time before she leaves for Cambodia. If she's going to earn CBE, she'll need to purchase the necessary review materials soon and really hit the books for the next couple of weeks.

Of course, there's no guarantee that Kaitlyn's score on the DSST exam will be high enough to earn CBE. So she needs to choose a course at State University as a backup plan. Of the four courses that satisfy the Fine Arts requirement, only History of Western Art plays to Kaitlyn's strengths and is definitely taught in her preferred format.

From her analysis, she knows that both History of Western Art instructors appear to grade favorably, awarding a high percentage of As and Bs, and that they distribute grades similarly. As a result, Kaitlyn doesn't prefer one instructor over the other. Had both instructors been drill sergeant graders, she might have wanted to look again at one or more of the courses she analyzed (and rejected) in Stage IV to see how those instructors typically grade. Thankfully, she doesn't need to do this.

Stage VII: Decide How to Fulfill Your Degree Plan Requirement

Kaitlyn has gathered all the information she needs to make an informed decision and has weighed her options for fulfilling the Fine Arts requirement. Now it's decision time.

For Kaitlyn, this isn't a difficult choice. Since she has little to lose by trying to earn CBE, she opts to first prepare on her own to pass the DSST exam before she leaves for Cambodia. If she earns a passing score, she'll get credit hours toward her degree for History of Western Art without having to take that course at all. If she doesn't earn CBE, her second choice will be to register for History of Western Art with either of the two instructors. If she happens to hear better things about one of the instructors, she'll try to register for that one.

Because this isn't the only degree plan requirement Kaitlyn will be analyzing, she needs to keep track of her decisions. To do this, Kaitlyn makes a list like the following:

Preference List to Fulfill Fine Arts Degree Plan Requirement	
1	Attempt to earn CBE for course History of Western Art with the DSST Art of the Western World exam. If unable to score high enough on that exam, then …
2	Take History of Western Art at State University with either Professor Young or Professor Zimmer.

It looks as though Kaitlyn is in a win-win situation. If she earns CBE, she'll receive credit hours for History of Western Art and can use the freed-up space in her first-semester schedule to fulfill another degree plan requirement. If she doesn't earn CBE, she'll take History of Western Art, a course that appears to be a great fit for her.

By investing a small amount of time to investigate her options through the GPAMaxx Course Selection Module, Kaitlyn has set the stage for her success.

CASE STUDY #2

Selecting Courses in Your Major

Josh, Tactical Freshman History Major

Josh is a history major in his second semester at State University. Soon he will need to register for his third-semester courses. He wants to find well-fitting courses that will help him maximize his GPA and fulfill degree requirements.

Next semester will be an especially busy one for Josh. He'll be pledging a fraternity and continuing to play on his water polo club team, so he won't have as much time as he'd like to spend on his coursework. Therefore, he'll need to seriously consider each potential course's time commitment. He won't want to enroll in courses that would likely require a disproportionately large amount of work.

To help him analyze his potential courses and select the ones to take, Josh will use the GPAMaxx Course Selection Module. He'll work through all seven stages of the GPAMaxx Course Selection Module to do this.

Stage I: Choose a Degree Plan Requirement and Discover Which Courses Fulfill It

Josh's degree plan requires him to complete at least one non–Western history course at State University by the end of next semester. Since Josh hasn't done this, he opts to analyze this requirement first.

Five courses offered next semester fulfill this requirement. They are:

- Ancient Egyptian Civilization, a 60-student lecture course taught by Professor Abdullah, who will base the final course grade on two term papers (each counting for 25 percent of the final course grade), and two equally weighted in-class essay exams (25 percent each).

- History of Japan to 1857, a small seminar taught by Professor Bell. The final grade is based on 10 essays, due on a near-weekly basis (8.5 percent each), and attendance and class participation (15 percent).

- History of India through Independence, an auditorium-size lecture course taught by Professor Cipriani. The final grade is based on three equally weighted in-class exams (one-third each) with both multiple-choice and essay components. No credit is awarded for class participation, but attendance is mandatory.

- South Africa's Boer War, a small seminar taught by Professor Dowling. The final grade is based on two term papers (35 percent each), a group project (20 percent), and attendance and class participation (10 percent).

- History of Dutch Colonization in Indonesia, a small seminar taught by Professor Engels, who bases the final grade on three term papers (30 percent each), and attendance and class participation (10 percent).

Now that he knows which courses fulfill the non–Western history course requirement, Josh makes a list of them and can begin gathering information about each one.

Stage II: Discover Your Credit by Examination (CBE) Options

Josh finds out if he can test out of any of these courses by earning CBE. Unfortunately, the answer is no. State University requires history majors to complete their single non–Western history course requirement by taking a course on campus.

Stage III: Discover Your Transfer Course Options

Because Josh must fulfill the non–Western history course requirement by taking a course at State University, this is not an option. He doesn't need to investigate his transfer course options.

Stage IV: Investigate Your Potential Courses

Now Josh needs to investigate each course that fulfills the non–Western history course requirement. For each course, he's trying to determine whether its subject plays to his academic strengths and if it's taught in his preferred format. Since he wants to select courses that are a good fit, he plans to initially screen out those that aren't. If a course doesn't play to his strengths, or its format doesn't seem well suited for him, he'd rather seek out an alternate course that appears to be a better fit. He'll analyze the screened-out courses beyond Stage IV only if all his other choices seem to be an equally bad or worse fit.

Before he starts investigating, Josh briefly reflects on his academic strengths and weaknesses and the type of instructional and grading formats that constitute his preferred format. Josh has an aptitude for history generally, having been a very strong student in his high school history classes and in his single history course at State University last semester. Many history topics interest him. That's a big reason he chose to major in it.

Although he's in only his second semester at State University, Josh is fortunate to already have a good idea of his preferred format for courses. He likes small seminar courses with extensive student and instructor interaction. He enjoys writing papers and doing research, working in groups, and making presentations to small groups of fellow students. He dislikes any type of time-pressured in-class exam. Josh doesn't feel comfortable in giant auditorium-size courses where he's one of hundreds of students—something he learned the hard way by taking a large lecture course last semester. Going forward, whenever it makes sense to do so, he wants to take small, writing-intensive courses without exams, taught by instructors who value participation and interaction.

Now Josh begins to analyze his course choices, starting with Ancient Egyptian Civilization. After reading a detailed course description, Josh concludes that this isn't the course for him. He simply doesn't have any interest in the ancient history of the region. He also prefers small class sizes. And the fact that half his grade in the course would be based on in-class exams is another big minus. Based on these factors, Josh opts to strike Ancient Egyptian Civilization from his list. If none of the other courses seems a better fit, he can always come back and look at this course in more detail.

Josh looks next at History of Japan to 1857. Compared to the other courses, this one, with near-weekly essays, will require a lot of work and a far greater overall time commitment. Not wanting to overload his schedule for next semester, Josh crosses this off his list—at least until he analyzes the remaining courses—without considering it further.

Next he turns to History of India through Independence. He likes the topic. In addition, the course seems unlikely to require a disproportionate amount of work.

But there are problems. First, the grading format. Josh doesn't like time-pressured exams, so the fact that three in-class exams make up the total course grade is a huge negative. Second, the instructional format. History of India through Independence is an auditorium-size lecture course, an instructional format far from Josh's preferred learning style. Not surprisingly, he opts to give this course a pass without analyzing it further and strikes it from his list.

Josh now has two courses left to analyze: South Africa's Boer War, taught by Professor Dowling, and History of Dutch Colonization in Indonesia, taught by Professor Engels. Both cover colonial history, a topic Josh finds interesting. Although both courses require multiple term papers, Josh concludes that neither class will require a disproportionate amount of work.

Both courses are small seminars, his ideal instructional format. And both are in his ideal grading format, with final grades based on term papers and class participation. In addition, Professor Dowling's class requires a group project. Josh does well on term papers and essays, thrives on group projects, and loves to participate in class. Because of its group project, Josh prefers the grading format of South Africa's Boer War, but the format of both courses seems a good fit.

Of all the courses he's analyzed, South Africa's Boer War and History of Dutch Colonization in Indonesia appear best suited for him. Because of this, Josh opts to analyze only these two courses further.

Stage V: Go Professor Shopping

Josh proceeds to professor shop South Africa's Boer War and History of Dutch Colonization in Indonesia to learn how the instructor teaching each one graded students during previous semesters. He finds a website that shows exactly how each instructor awarded grades for this course in recent semesters. Here's the breakdown of grades for each instructor:

Professor Dowling, South Africa's Boer War

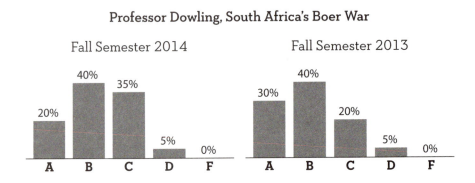

Professor Engels, History of Dutch Colonization in Indonesia

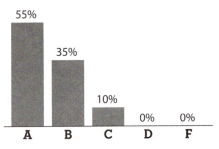

Professor Engels has taught this course only once before, and Josh fears that the grades he awarded in fall 2014 may not be consistent with his usual grading tendencies. Because Josh is uncomfortable evaluating the professor on just one data point, he also looks at Professor Engels' grade distribution histories in a similar course.

He finds a seminar Professor Engels taught in fall 2013, History of French Colonization in Indochina. Josh determines that this course is similar in size, format, and audience, so it will give him a reasonable idea of Professor Engels' grading tendencies in the course Josh is now considering. And indeed, Professor Engels' grading pattern in this class is very similar to his record in History of Dutch Colonization in Indonesia.

Professor Engels, History of French Colonization in Indochina

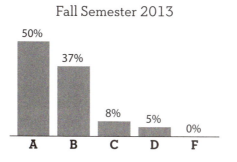

Fall Semester 2013

Based on their past grade distributions in identical or similar courses, Professor Engels seems to be a more favorable grader than Professor Dowling. Professor Engels gave an A to at least half of his students in each of those seminars and awarded higher grades overall.

Stage VI: Weigh Your Options to Fulfill Your Degree Plan Requirement

Now Josh must weigh all his options to fulfill the non–Western history course requirement. He's narrowed his choices down to South Africa's Boer War and History of Dutch Colonization in Indonesia.

Based solely on the format of the course, South Africa's Boer War, with its group project, would be Josh's first choice. However, Josh may find it harder to earn an A, because the instructor, Professor Dowling, seems likely to award lower grades than Professor Engels will in History of Dutch Colonization in Indonesia. Josh finds the format of Professor Engels' course slightly less favorable, but he's still very comfortable with it. And since Josh wants to take the course that offers him the best shot to maximize his GPA, finding the instructor who grades more favorably is important.

Stage VII: Decide How to Fulfill Your Degree Plan Requirement

Josh has gathered all the information he needs to make an informed decision and has weighed his options to fulfill the non–Western history course requirement. Now it's decision time.

Ultimately, Josh selects as his first-choice course the one he believes will give him the best chance to earn an A, History of Dutch Colonization in Indonesia. In the event that course is already filled when he registers, his backup plan is to take South Africa's Boer War.

Because this isn't the only degree plan requirement Josh will be analyzing, he needs to keep track of his decisions. To do this, Josh makes a list like the following:

Preference List to Fulfill Non-Western History Course Requirement	
1	Take History of Dutch Colonization in Indonesia with Professor Engels. If Professor Engel's course is already full, then ...
2	Take South Africa's Boer War with Professor Dowling.

By using the GPAMaxx Course Selection Module to analyze his course options, Josh found a first-choice course that is all of the following: well suited to his strengths, focused on a topic that interests him, unlikely to require a disproportionate amount of work, taught in his preferred format, and with an instructor who has graded favorably in past semesters.

He had to think strategically and weigh competing variables to reach a decision. Based on the professors' grading histories, the course taught in his first-choice format didn't seem to offer Josh the best chance for an A. Instead, his top choice was the course with a slightly less favorable format, but with an instructor who has graded more favorably in the past.

This is exactly the kind of strategic trade-off you may have to make as you select your courses. If the variables had been different, Josh might have made a different choice. When you evaluate any course, always measure the variables and think strategically to reach your decisions, just as Josh did.

Make no mistake: Josh will have to work hard in his first-choice course if he wants to earn a good grade. But by investing a small amount of time to investigate his options through the GPAMaxx Course Selection Module, Josh has set the stage for his success.

RESOURCES

Providing you with information about individual universities is beyond the size and scope of this book.

As a first step, though, we provide the web addresses of some general resources for current and future public university students. Although these websites serve as a starting point for gathering information on your own, be aware that they vary enormously in both their content and potential usefulness.

These are not exhaustive lists. Many other websites may be helpful, so don't confine your searches to these websites alone. Furthermore, web addresses change fairly regularly. If you are unable to locate these websites at the addresses below, search for their updated URLs.

Credit by Examination

Advanced Placement (AP)
(http://apcentral.collegeboard.com/home)

Cambridge Advanced International Certificate of Education
(Cambridge AICE)
(http://www.cie.org.uk/programmes-and-qualifications/cambridge-advanced/
cambridge-aice-diploma/)

College Level Examination Program (CLEP)
(http://clep.collegeboard.org/)

DANTES Subject Standardized Tests (DSST)
(http://www.getcollegecredit.com)

Excelsior Examination Program
(https://www.excelsior.edu/exams)

International Baccalaureate (IB)
(http://www.ibo.org)

Transfer Coursework

Many (but not all) states maintain individual websites that help the
state's current and future public university students with transfer
courses and transfer-related issues. Here are some of them:

Alabama
Statewide Transfer and Articulation Reporting System (STARS)
(http://stars.troy.edu/)

Alaska
University of Alaska Student Transfer Credit Resource Site
(https://uaonline.alaska.edu/banprod/owa/bwsk2tcr.P_Tcs_Selmau)

Arizona
Az Transfer
(http://aztransfer.com)

Arkansas
Arkansas Course Transfer System (ACTS)
(http://acts.adhe.edu/)

California
Articulation System Stimulating Interinstitutional Student Transfer (ASSIST)
(www.assist.org)

Colorado
Colorado Department of Higher Education
(http://highered.colorado.gov/Academics/Transfers/Students.html)

Connecticut
Connecticut State Colleges and Universities, Board of Regents for Higher
    Education, Transfer
(http://www.ct.edu/admission/transfers)

Florida
State University System of Florida
(http://www.flbog.edu/forstudents/ati/transfer.php)

Georgia
Georgia Transfer Articulation Cooperative Services (GAtracs)
(https://secure.gacollege411.org/College_Planning/GATRACS/
    Transfer_Student_Planner.aspx)

Hawaii
The University of Hawaii System, UH System Transfer Course Database
(http://www.hawaii.edu/transferdatabase/)

Idaho
Idaho State Board of Education, Public College and University Transfer
    Equivalency Guides
(http://www.boardofed.idaho.gov/public_col_univ/credit_transfer.asp)

Illinois
iTransfer
(http://www.itransfer.org)

Indiana
State of Indiana Official Source for Course Transfer Information
(http://www.transferin.net)

Iowa
Transfer In Iowa
(http://www.transferiniowa.org/agreements.php)

Kansas
Kansas Board of Regents, Transfer and Articulation
(http://www.kansasregents.org/transfer_articulation)

Kentucky
Kentucky Council on Postsecondary Education, Transfer Policies and Initiatives
(http://cpe.ky.gov/policies/academicinit/transfer/)

Louisiana
Transfer Degree Guarantee
(http://latransferdegree.org/)

Maine
University of Maine System, Transfer Course Equivalencies
(http://www.maine.edu/transfer-students/transfer-course-equivalencies/)

Maryland
The Articulation System for Maryland Colleges and Universities (ARTSYS)
(http://artsys.usmd.edu/transferinfo.html)

Massachusetts
MassTransfer
(http://www.mass.edu/masstransfer/)

Michigan
Michigan Transfer Network
(http://www.michigantransfernetwork.org/)

Minnesota
Minnesota Transfer
(http://www.mntransfer.org/)

Mississippi
Mississippi Articulation and Transfer Tool (MATT)
(http://www.mississippi.edu/trnms/about/splash.aspx)

Missouri
Missouri Department of Higher Education, Credit Transfer
(http://dhe.mo.gov/cota/credittransfermain.php)

Montana
Montana University System Transfer
(http://mus.edu/Transfer/transfer.asp)

Nevada
Nevada System of Higher Education, Students: Transfer
(http://system.nevada.edu/Nshe/index.cfm/administration/
  academics-student-affairs/students/transfer/)

New Hampshire
NHTransfer
(http://www.nhtransfer.org/)

New Jersey
NJ Transfer
(http://www.njtransfer.org/)

New Mexico
New Mexico Higher Education Department,
  General Ed Core Course Transfer Curriculum
(http://www.hed.state.nm.us/institutions/general-ed-core-course
  -transfer-curriculum.aspx)

North Carolina
College Foundation of North Carolina
(http://www.cfnc.org/TransferNav)

North Dakota
North Dakota University System
(http://www.ndus.edu/employees/articulation-transfer/)

Ohio
Ohio Higher Ed, Credit Transfer
(http://www.ohiohighered.org/transfer)

Oklahoma
Oklahoma State Regents for Higher Education, Student Transfer Policies
(http://www.okhighered.org/transfer-students/policies.shtml)

Pennyslvania
Pennsylvania Transfer and Articulation Center (PA TRAC)
(http://www.pacollegetransfer.com/)

Rhode Island
RI Transfers
(http://www.ritransfers.org/)

South Carolina
South Carolina Transfer and Articulation Center (SC TRAC)
(https://www.sctrac.org/)

South Dakota
Select Dakota
(http://www.selectdakota.org/collegetransfer/)

Texas
Texas Common Course Numbering System
(http://www.tccns.org/)

Utah
TransferUtah
(http://www.transferutah.org/)

Virginia
State Council of Higher Education for Virginia (SCHEV), Transfer Tool
(http://www.schev.edu/students/transfer/default.asp)

Wisconsin
University of Wisconsin System, Transfer Information System
(http://tis.uwsa.edu/transfer/)

State-Supported College Information Websites

Many (but not all) states have websites that provide information relating to public university education and planning. Here are some of them:

Alabama
Alabama Commission on Higher Education
(http://www.ache.state.al.us/Default.aspx)

Alaska
Alaska Career Information System (AKCIS)
(https://acpe.alaska.gov/STUDENT-PARENT/College_Career/AKCIS)

Arizona
Arizona College Access Network (AzCAN)
(https://azcan.az.gov/)

Arizona Commission for Postsecondary Education
(http://www.azhighered.gov/)

Arkansas
Arkansas Department of Higher Education
(http://www.adhe.edu/students/Pages/students.aspx#2)

Fund My Future
(http://www.fundmyfuture.info)

California
Californiacolleges.edu
(http://www.californiacolleges.edu/)

Colorado
Colorado Department of Education
(http://highered.colorado.gov/dhedefault.html)

Connecticut
Connecticut State Colleges and Universities,
    Board of Regents for Higher Education
(http://www.ct.edu/)

Florida
College and Beyond
(http://www.fldoe.org/students/college.asp)

Georgia
GAcollege411
(http://www.gacollege411.org)

Hawaii
The University of Hawaii System
(http://www.hawaii.edu/)

Idaho
Idaho State Board of Education, Public Colleges and Universities
(http://www.boardofed.idaho.gov/public_col_univ/public_col_univ_jump.asp)

Illinois
Illinois Board of Higher Education
(http://www.ibhe.org/)

Indiana
Indiana Commission for Higher Education
(http://www.in.gov/che/)

Iowa
I Have A Plan Iowa
(https://secure.ihaveaplaniowa.gov/College_Planning/_default.aspx)

Kansas
The Kansas Board of Regents
(http://www.kansasregents.org/)

Kentucky
Kentucky Council on Postsecondary Education
(http://cpe.ky.gov/)

Louisiana
Louisiana Board of Regents
(http://regents.louisiana.gov/about-regents/colleges-amp-universities/)

Maine
College in Maine!
(http://www.mecolleges.org/)

Maryland
Maryland Higher Education Commission
(http://www.mhec.state.md.us/)

MD go 4 it
(http://www.mdgo4it.org/)

Massachusetts
Massachusetts Department of Higher Education,
    Information and Tools for Students
(http://www.mass.edu/forstudents/forstudents.asp)

Michigan
Michigan College Access Portal (MichiganCAP)
(https://www.michigancap.org/)

Minnesota
Minnesota State Colleges and Universities
(http://www.mnscu.edu/)

Missouri
Missouri Connections
(http://www.missouriconnections.org/)

Montana
Montana University System
(http://mus.edu/)

Nebraska
Education Quest Foundation
(http://www.educationquest.org/)

Nevada
Nevada System of Higher Education
(http://system.nevada.edu/Nshe/)

New Hampshire
NH Higher Education Assistance Foundation
(http://www.nhheaf.org/index.asp)

New Jersey
State of New Jersey, Office of the Secretary of Higher Education
(http://www.nj.gov/highereducation/)

New Mexico
New Mexico Higher Education Department, Students and Parents Overview
(http://www.hed.state.nm.us/students/)

New York
New York State Higher Education Services Corporation,
    Preparing for College
(http://www.hesc.ny.gov/prepare-for-college.html)

North Carolina
College Foundation of North Carolina
(https://www1.cfnc.org/My_CFNC/_default.aspx)

North Dakota
North Dakota University System
(http://ndus.edu/)

Ohio
Ohio Higher Ed
(http://www.ohiohighered.org/)

Oklahoma
OKcollegestart.org
(https://secure.okcollegestart.org/)

Oklahoma State Regents for Higher Education
(http://www.okhighered.org/)

Oregon
Oregon University System
(http://www.ous.edu/)

Pennsylvania
Pennsylvania Department of Education
(http://www.portal.state.pa.us/portal/server.pt/community/
    higher_education/8711/college_planning)

Rhode Island
Rhode Island Board of Governors for Higher Education
(http://www.ribghe.org/)

South Carolina
South Carolina Commission on Higher Education
(http://www.che.sc.gov/)

South Dakota
Select Dakota
(http://www.selectdakota.org/)

Tennessee
CollegeforTN.org
(https://secure.collegefortn.org/)

Texas
College For All Texans
(http://www.collegeforalltexans.com/)

Utah
Utah System of Higher Education
(http://www.higheredutah.org/)

Vermont

Vermont Student Assistance Corp.
(http://vsac.org)

Virginia

I am the One
(http://www.i-am-the-one.com/)

Virginia Education Wizard
(https://www.vawizard.org/)

West Virginia

College Foundation of West Virginia
(http://www.cfwv.com)

Wisconsin

University of Wisconsin System
(https://www.wisconsin.edu/)

Wyoming

WYO4Ed
(http://www.wyo4ed.org/)

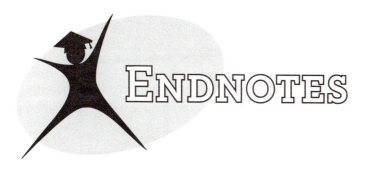

ENDNOTES

1   U.S. Department of Education, National Center for Education Statistics, Integrated Postsecondary Data System (IPEDS), Spring 2011, Graduation Rates component, in Laura G. Knapp, Janice E. Kelly-Reid, Scott A. Ginder, RTI International, *Enrollment in Postsecondary Institutions, Fall 2010; Financial Statistics, Fiscal Year 2010*; and *Graduation Rates, Selected Cohorts, 2002–07* (March 2012), 19.

2   FICO, *Is Growing Student Loan Debt Impacting Credit Risk?* FICO Insights, Number 65 (January 2013), 2.

3   *NACE Research: Job Outlook 2012*, National Association of Colleges and Employers (November 2011), 24.

4   Hope Yen, "1 in 2 Graduates Are Jobless or Underemployed," Associated Press, April 23, 2012. http://finance.yahoo.com/news/ 1-2-graduates-jobless-underemployed-140300522.html. See also Caroline Porter, "College Diplomas, With a Side of Specialized Study," *The Wall Street Journal*, November 21, 2014. http://online.wsj.com/ articles/college-diplomas-with-a-side-of-specialized-study-141658926.

5   Linda DeAngelo, Ray Franke, Sylvia Hurtado, John H. Pryor, Serge Tran, *Completing College: Assessing Graduation Rates at Four-Year Institutions* (Los Angeles: Higher Education Research Institute, UCLA, 2011), 15.

6   ACT Research and Policy Issues, *National Collegiate Retention and Persistence to Degree Rates* (2012), 4–5. http://www.act.org/research/ policymakers/pdf/retain_2012.pdf.

7   U.S. Department of Education, 19.

8   Sandy Baum and Jennifer Ma, *Trends in College Pricing 2014*, The College Board Trends in Higher Education Series (2014), 3, 12. https://secure-media.collegeboard.org/digitalServices/misc/trends/ 2014-trends-college-pricing-report-final.pdf.

9   University of Virginia, Student Financial Services, *Estimated Cost of Attendance for Undergraduate Students*, 2014–2015 (2014). http://sfs.virginia.edu/14-15 (retrieved 2014).

10   PayScale, Inc., *2013–14 PayScale College Salary Report*, State
     Schools by Salary Potential (2013). http://www.payscale.com/
     college-salary-report-2014/best-schools-by-type/state-schools.

11   Rich Robbins, "Advisor Load," in Aaron H. Carlstrom, ed., 2011
     NACADA National Survey of Academic Advising, National Academic
     Advising Association, Clearinghouse of Academic Advising Resources.
     http://www.nacada.ksu.edu (retrieved 2013). Statistic refers only to
     public universities that award doctoral degrees.

12   *Time is the Enemy*, Complete College America (September 2011), 12.
     http://www.completecollege.org/docs/Time_Is_the_Enemy.pdf.

13   David Leibow, *The Number One Cause of College Unhappiness*,
     Psychology Today, September 2, 2010. http://www.psychologytoday
     .com/print/47392.

14   Yen, April 23, 2012.

15   *NACE Research*, 24.

16   Jonathan Gemus, *College Achievement and Earnings, Working Paper
     2010:9*, Uppsala Center for Labor Studies, Department of Economics,
     Uppsala University (2010), 2, 4–5, 30.

17   Stuart Rojstaczer, and Christopher Healy, *Grading in American
     Colleges and Universities*, Teachers College Record, March 4, 2010.
     http://www.tcrecord.org/PrintContent.asp?ContentID=15928;
     Stuart Rojstaczer, "Grade inflation gone wild," The Christian Science
     Monitor, March 24, 2009. http://www.csmonitor.com/Commentary/
     Opinion/2009/0324/p09s02-coop.html.

18   Dave Breitenstein, "Fla. Colleges: Good grades, bad faith?," *The
     News-Press* (Fort Myers, Fla.), June 15, 2009, A1–A2.

19   David T. Conley, *College and Career Ready: Helping All Students
     Succeed Beyond High School* (San Francisco: Jossey-Bass, 2010), 30.

20   Eileen M. O'Brien and Chuck Dervarics, *Is high school tough enough*,
     The Center for Public Education (March 2012). http://www.centerfor
     publiceducation.org/Main-Menu/Instruction/Is-high-school-tough
     -enough-At-a-glance/Is-high-school-tough-enough-Full-report.html.

21   The College Board, "About the Exams." http://professionals.collegeboard
     .com/testing/ap/about.

22   The College Board, "Put AP to Work for You." https://apstudent.college
     board.org/exploreap/the-rewards.

23   D. D. Guttenplan, "A Newcomer Makes Good in the Credentials Market," The New York Times, July 3, 2011.

24   The College Board, "CLEP Information for Parents." http://clep.college board.org/parents-info.

25   DSST, "About DSST." http://getcollegecredit.com/about/.

26   See, for example, Wade Curry, Walt MacDonald, Rick Morgan, "The Advanced Placement Program: Access to Excellence," *Journal of Secondary Gifted Education,* Volume 11, Issue 1 (Fall 1999); Nancy K. Scammacca and Barbara G. Dodd, "An Investigation of Educational Outcomes for Students Who Earn College Credit Through the College-Level Examination Program," *College Board Research Report No. 2005–5* (2005), 1, 16, 18; Brad Moulder, Abdulbaset Abdulla, Deanna L. Morgan, "Validity and Fairness of CLEP Exams," *College Board Research Notes RN-22* (September 2005), 4–6; Rick Morgan and John Klaric, "AP Students in College: An Analysis of Five-Year Academic Careers," *College Board Research Report No. 2007–4* (2007), 4, 9; Leslie Keng and Barbara G. Dodd, "A Comparison of College Performances of AP and Non-AP Student Groups in 10 Subject Areas," *College Board Research Report No. 2008–7* (2008), 1, 17, 18.

27   See, for example, Nancy K. Scammacca and Barbara G. Dodd, "An Investigation of Educational Outcomes for Students Who Earn College Credit Through the College-Level Examination Program," *College Board Research Report No. 2005–5* (2005), 1, 16, 18; Linda Hargrove, Donn Godin, Barbara G. Dodd, "College Outcomes Comparisons by AP and Non-AP High School Experiences," *College Board Research Report No. 2008–3* (2008), 1, 47–48; Leslie Keng and Barbara G. Dodd, "A Comparison of College Performances of AP and Non-AP Student Groups in 10 Subject Areas," *College Board Research Report No. 2008–7* (2008), 1, 17, 18.

28   The College Board, "Percentage of Schools Offering Dual Enrollment," The College Completion Agenda. http://completionagenda.collegeboard .org/percentage-schools-offering-dual-enrollment.

29   Ben Struhl and Joel Vargas, "Taking College Courses in High School: A Strategy for College Readiness," Jobs for the Future (October 2012), vi, 11, 17; Crystal Collins, "Redesigning Dual Enrollment to Promote College Completion," *SREB Policy Brief,* Southern Regional Education Board (February 2012), 2–3; Joni L. Swanson, "An analysis of the impact of high school dual enrollment course participation on post-secondary academic success, persistence and degree completion," presented at the meeting of the National Association for Gifted Children, Tampa,

Fla., and the National Alliance of Concurrent Enrollment Partnerships, Kansas City, Mo. (2008), 4; Wesley R. Habley, Jennifer L. Bloom, and Steve Robbins, *Increasing Persistence: Research-Based Strategies for College Student Success* (San Francisco: Jossey-Bass, 2012), 121–122.

30   For a good overview of student evaluations and some of their shortcomings and benefits, see Philip B. Stark and Richard Freishtat, *An Evaluation of Course Evaluations*, University of California, Berkeley (September 2014). http://www.stat.berkeley.edu/~stark/Preprints/evaluations14.pdf.

INDEX

A

Abitur, 110
academic advisors
  caseloads of, 25
  conflicts of interest of, 27–28
  GPA maximization vs., 26–27
  introduction to, 23–24
  limits on knowledge of, 26, 80
  personalized awareness and,
    25–26
  working with, 28
academic calendars, 33
Academic Earth, 126
academic strengths/weaknesses
  case studies of, 234–235, 242
  determining, 159–163
  in GPAMaxx Course Selection
    Module, 218–219
  introduction to, 153–154
ACCUPLACER® exams, 103
ACT exams, 103, 161
Advanced Placement (AP) program
  case studies of, 117–119, 122
  credit by examination and,
    103–104, 129–130
  dual enrollment and, 135–137
  for exam subjects, 104
  in university game plans, 196–203
A-levels, 110
anecdotal information, 180–181
AP (Advanced Placement)
    programs. *See* Advanced
    Placement (AP) programs
aptitude for majors, 92–93. *See*
    also academic strengths/
    weaknesses

articulation agreements, 134–135
associate's degrees, 195. *See also*
    community colleges
auditorium-size courses, 88,
    155, 166. *See also* ideal
    instructional formats
avoiding difficult courses. *See*
    difficult degree requirements

B

Baccalauréate, 110

C

Cambridge Advanced International
    Certificate of Education, 103
Cardinal Rules. *See* GPAMaxx
    Cardinal Rules.
  AP exams in, 117–119, 122, 139
caseloads of advisors, 25
CBE (credit by examination). *See*
    credit by examination (CBE)
class rank, 61–64, 68–71
class size, 88–89, 155, 166. *See*
    also instructional formats
CLEP (College-Level Examination
    Program). *See* College-Level
    Examination Program (CLEP)
College Board, 104, 107
College-Level Examination
    Program (CLEP)
  availability of, 104
  case studies of, 117–119, 139
  credit and, 105–107
  for exam subjects, 105–106
  in university game plans,
    198–203

community colleges, 140–141,
    145–203
COMPASS® exams, 103
conflicts of interest, 27–28
contracts
    articulation agreements as,
        134–135
    degree plans as, 81
cost of education
    credit by examination and, 112,
        119–120
    degree plans and, 78
    timely vs. late graduation and,
        21–22
    transfer courses and, 142
course credit by examination. *See*
    credit by examination (CBE)
course loads
    credit by examination and, 113,
        120
    transfer courses and, 138, 142
course registration. *See*
    registration, priority for
course requirements. *See* degree
    plans
Course Selection Module. *See*
    GPAMaxx Course Selection
    Module
Coursera, 127
courses, transferring credit for.
    See transfer courses
credit by examination (CBE)
    action plans for, 202–203
    Advanced Placement for,
        103–104, 129–130
    advantages of, generally,
        112–116
    case studies of, 117–123, 139,
        237–239, 241
    CLEP exams for, 105–107
    course selection and, 223–224
    in degree plans, 87–88
    difficult degree requirements
        via, 114–115

DSST exams for, 107–108
early graduation via, 113,
    119–120
electives via, 132
general education courses via,
    130–131
in GPAMaxx Course Selection
    Module, 214–215, 233, 241
GPAs and, 114–115, 120, 124
IB program for, 105, 129–130
international students and, 110
introduction to, 99, 101–102
introductory requirements via,
    121–123, 130–132
lighter course loads via, 113, 120
multiple exams on same subject
    for, 130
national exam programs for, 103
nonelective degree requirements
    via, 132
online courses for, 126–127
order of taking exams for,
    128–132
pitfalls of, 121–124
preparing for, 125–127
prioritizing use of, 128–132
priority for course registration
    via, 115–116, 121
resources on, 250
rules/policies governing, 84
saving money via, 112, 119–120
scores in, 114–115, 146
study guides for, 126
timely graduation via, 113, 120
timing of tests for, 128
transfer courses and, 144,
    146–148
types of exams for, 102–109
in university game plans,
    193–194, 196–203
university-specific exams for,
    109
weakest subjects via, 130–131,
    145–146

credit hours
  credit by examination and, 124
  degree plans and, 81, 83
  distribution requirements and, 87
  dual enrollment and, 136–137
  GPAs and, 40–41
  grades and, 34–36
  rules/policies governing, 83
  transfer courses and, 134
Credit/No Credit grades, 33
criteria-based grading, 56–58
cum laude, 63
cumulative GPAs (grade point averages)
  GPA-based honors and, 63
  introduction to, 37–39
  transfer courses and, 134, 145–146
current university students, 11
curved grading, 54–56, 89
cutoffs, 64–67

D
DANTES Subject Standardized Tests (DSST)
  availability of, 104
  case studies of, 117–119, 122, 233–238
  for credit by examination, 107–108
  for exam subjects, 107–108
  introduction to, 103
Darwinism, 58
degree plans
  advantages of understanding, 80–81
  blunders to avoid in navigating, 78–79
  as contracts, 81
  credit by examination in. *See* credit by examination (CBE)
  dissecting, generally, 83
  distributions in, 86–88

elective courses in, 93–95
general education requirements in, 85–90
GPAMaxx Cardinal Rule for, 21, 75
honors programs in, 96–97
introduction to, 75
majors in, 90–93
minors in, 90–93
online coursework in, 95–96
rules/policies governing, 83–84
sample of, 76–78
transfer courses in. *See* transfer courses
university road maps for, 9, 75
degree requirements
  difficult. *See* difficult degree requirements
  elective, 93–95, 132
  general education. *See* general education requirements
  introductory, 130–132
  nonelective, 132
  time-intensive, 92
demystifying grade game. *See* grades
difficult degree requirements. *See also* academic strengths/weaknesses
  credit by examination for, 114–115
  GPAs and, 166
Distinction/High Distinction/Highest Distinction honors, 63
distributions, 86–88
drill sergeant grading
  in general education courses, 89
  in grading practices, 57
  professor shopping and, 171–172
DSST (DANTES Subject Standardized Tests). *See* DANTES Subject Standardized Tests (DSST)
dual enrollment, 135–137, 196

E

early graduation
credit by examination for, 113, 119–120
transfer courses for, 137, 142
grading and, generally, 29
Education Portal, 126
edX, 127
electives, 93–95, 132
employment
GPAs impacting, 42, 48–49, 62
internships and, 47
long-term earnings, 49
private vs. public universities and, 50
statistics on, 4–5
strategy for, 6
exam preparation to earn CBE, 125–127
examples. *See* case studies
Excelsior College Examinations, 103
excess credit hours, 34
extracurricular activities
credit by examination and, 113
degree plans and, 81
GPAs and, 46–47
transfer courses and, 138

F

foreign languages, 123, 198
foreign students, 110
France, 110
free online courses, 126–127
Fulbright scholarships, 232

G

Game Plan Module. *See* GPAMaxx Game Plan Module
general education requirements
class size and, 88–89
credit by examination for, 130–131
distributions in, 86–88
interest level and, 90
introduction to, 85–86
pitfalls of, 88–90
stringent grading in, 89
transition to college and, 89
Germany, 110
GPA hurdle rates, 48
GPA-based honors
class rank in, 64, 68–71
examples of, 64–71
GPA cutoffs in, 64–70
grade replacement policies and, 42
institutional GPA cutoffs in, 65–70
introduction to, 61–62
levels of, 63
university standards for, 62–64
GPAMaxx Cardinal Rules
overview of, 21–22
on professor shopping. *See* professor shopping
on self-awareness. *See* knowing yourself as student
on university road maps. *See* degree plans
GPAMaxx Course Selection Module
benefits of, 229
credit by examination in, 214–215, 233, 241
degree requirement decisions in, 226–228, 238–239, 246–247
degree requirement options in, 222–225, 237–238, 246
degree requirements in, generally, 213–214, 232–233, 240–241
general education requirements in, 231–239
introduction to, 20, 209–210
investigating course options in, 218–219, 234–236, 242–244
majors in, 240–247

professor shopping in, 220–221,
236–237, 244–245
transfer courses in, 216–218,
234, 241
using, generally, 210–212
GPAMaxx Game Plan Module
alternative methods for credits
in, 200–205
beneficiaries of, 189–190
credit by examination in,
202–203
current knowledge in, 198–199
current position in, 196–197
early graduation and, 188–189
introduction to, 18–19, 185
majors and, 187
need for, 186–189
rules/policies governing degrees
in, 193–195
transfer courses in, 204–205
for two-year colleges, 195
university master game plans in,
191–192, 206–208
using, generally, 190–191
GPAMaxx Strategy
overview of, 9, 12, 15–18
perspectives in, 7–8
planning degree programs in.
See Game Plan Module
rules in. See GPAMaxx Cardinal
Rules
selecting courses in. See GPAMaxx
Course Selection Module
solutions in, 8
GPAs (grade point averages). See
also grades
academic advisors and, 26–27
bad grades impacting, 39–41
college experience and, 46–47
credit by examination and,
114–115, 120, 124, 145-146
credit hours and, 35–36
cumulative. See cumulative GPAs
(grade point averages)

difficult degree requirements
and, 114–115, 137–138, 166
employers and, 48–49
Game Plan Module for. See
GPAMaxx Game Plan Module
grade inflation and, 50–51
grade replacement policies and,
42–43
graduate school and, 49
honors based on. See GPA-based
honors
impact of bad grades on, 39–41
impact of, generally, 45–49
institutional. See institutional
GPAs (grade point averages)
letter grading, 32
long-term earnings and, 49
overview of, 31, 36
at private vs. public universities,
50
university grading practices and.
See grading practices
grade distribution histories
case studies of, 173–174,
236–237, 244–245
comparisons of, 177
course formats and, 177
in course selection, 220–221
introduction to, 172
limitations of, 174
locating, 175–176
reviewing, 176, 178–182
grade inflation, 50–51
grade point averages (GPAs). See
GPAs (grade point averages)
grade points, defined, 31
grade replacement policies, 41–43
grades. See also GPAs (grade point
averages)
credit hours and, 34–36
impact of bad, 39–41
introduction to, 9, 29
letters as, 32
pass-fail, 33, 94

grades (*continued*)
replacement policies for, 42–43
semester vs. quarter systems
and, 33
university grading practices for.
See grading practices
grading formats
case studies of, 234–236,
242–244
preferred course formats and,
154–157, 164–165
grading on the curve, 54–56, 89,
139
grading practices
criteria-based grading in, 56–58
curved grading in, 54–56, 89
drill sergeant grading in, 57
impact of, 59
introduction to, 53–54
measured grading in, 57–58
by specific professors. *See* grade
distribution histories
weed-out courses in, 58
graduate schools
cumulative GPAs and, 37–38,
145–146
GPAs impacting admittance to,
generally, 49–50
grade replacement policies and,
42
positioning for, 4–6, 8, 49
graduation
early. *See* early graduation
with GPA-based honors. *See*
GPA-based honors
late, 2, 15–16, 21–22
requirements for. *See* degree
plans
on time. *See* timely graduation

H
high schools
advanced placement courses
in, 103

college courses in, 135–137
credit by examination and,
129–130
dual enrollment in, 135–137
use of book for students still in,
10–11
grading formats in, 164
honors programs, 46, 96–97. *See
also* GPA-based honors
Honors/High Honors/Highest
Honors, 63

I
IB (International Baccalaureate)
program. *See* International
Baccalaureate (IB) program
ideal grading formats, 156–157,
166. *See also* grading
formats
ideal instructional formats
case studies of, 235–236,
242–243
class size and, 155, 166
determining, 164–166
introduction to, 155–157
preferences for, 154–157
"inner student." *See* knowing
yourself as student
institutional GPA cutoffs, 65–70
institutional GPAs (grade point
averages)
GPA-based honors and,
generally, 61–65
GPA-based honors at specific
universities, 65–70
introduction to, 36–39
transfer courses and, 37, 134,
137–138, 141–145
instructional formats
case studies of, 237, 243
class size and, 88–89, 155, 166
determining, 164–166
introduction to, 155–157
preferences for, 154–157

interest levels
    general education requirements
        and, 90
    "like" factor and, 167
    majors and, 92–93
International Baccalaureate (IB)
    program
    credit by examination and, 105,
        129–130
international students, 110
internet research
    on course subjects, 163
    for grade distribution histories,
        176, 179–182, 236, 244
Italy, 110

J
jobs. See employment

K
knowing yourself as student
    GPAMaxx Cardinal Rule for, 21,
        151–152
    ideal grading formats in, 156, 166
    introduction to, 9, 149, 151–152
    "like" factor in, 167
    preferred course formats in,
        154–157, 159, 164–166
    steps toward, 153
    strengths and weaknesses in,
        153–154, 159–163
    time of day and, 156
    workloads and, 157
koofers.com, 176

L
late graduation, 2, 15–16, 21–22
left-handedness, 151
letter grades, 32, 124
levels of GPA-based honors, 63
lighter course loads
    credit by examination enabling,
        113, 120
    transfer courses for, 138, 142

"like" factor, 167
limited course choices, 92
loads
    credit by examination and, 113,
        120
    transfer courses and, 138, 142
long-term earnings, 49
lower-division courses, 87

M
magna cum laude, 63, 192
majors
    aptitude/interest level for,
        92–93
    credit by examination and, 116,
        121
    in degree plans, 90–93
    in GPAMaxx Course Selection
        Module, 240–247
    introduction to, 90–91
    limited choice of courses for,
        92
    pitfalls of, 92–93
    requirements for, 91
    time-intensive commitment to,
        92
massive open online courses
    (MOOCs), 127
mathematics, 106, 108. See also
    STEM (Science, Technology,
    Engineering and Math)
Maturita, 110
measured grading, 57–58, 172
minors
    in degree plans, 90–93
    introduction to, 90–91
    limited choice of courses for, 92
    pitfalls of, 92–93
    requirements for, 91
MOOCs (massive open online
    courses), 127
morning courses, 156
multiple exams that test same
    subject, 130

multiple-choice format
in AP exams, 103
in CLEP exams, 106
in DSST exams, 107
essays vs., 152, 177
in ideal grading formats, 156,
164–165
myedu.com, 176

N
National Association of Colleges
and Employers, 48
national exam, for high school
equivalency, 110
national exam programs, 103
need for planning. *See* planning
numerical grades, 32

O
online coursework
for credit by examination, 126
in degree plans, 95–96
rules/policies governing, 84
in university game plans, 194
online forums, 180–181
Open Courseware Consortium,
126
order of exams for credit,
128–129

P
parents, 12
pass-fail grades
credit by examination and, 115,
145–146
elective courses and, 94
in university game plans,
193–194
overview of, 33
personalized awareness of
advisors, 25–26
Phi Beta Kappa, 192
policies of universities, 83–84
preference lists, 228, 239, 246

preferred course formats, 164–166.
See also ideal instructional
format and ideal grading
format
preparing for exams to earn credit
by examination, 125–127
prerequisites, 91, 187, 188–189
prioritizing credit by examination,
128–132
priority for course registration
credit by examination and,
115–116, 121
transfer courses and, 138–139,
142–143
private vs. public university
students, 50
professor shopping
case studies of, 173–174,
236–237, 244–245
in Course Selection Module,
220–221, 236–237, 244–245
GPAMaxx Cardinal Rule for, 21,
171–172
grading patterns in. *See* grade
distribution histories
guidelines for, 178–182
introduction to, 9, 169, 171–172
limitations of, 172, 174
steps in, 175–177
students withdrawing from
courses and, 181–182
tips for, 178–182
tutorial on, 175–182

Q
quarter vs. semester systems, 33

R
ratemyprofessors.com, 180
registration, priority for
credit by examination and,
115–116, 121
transfer courses and, 138–139,
142–143

resources
  on credit by examination, 250
  state-supported college
    information websites, 254–258
  on transfer courses, 250–254
right-handedness, 151

S
SAT, 103, 161
SAT Subject Tests, 103
Satisfactory/Unsatisfactory grades,
  33
saving money. *See also* cost of
  education
  credit by examination for, 112
  real dollar cost, 119–120
  transfer courses for, 142
science, 93, 106. *See also* STEM
  (Science, Technology,
  Engineering and Math)
self-evaluations, 152, 159–167.
  See also knowing yourself as
  student
semester vs. quarter systems, 33
size of classes, 88–89, 155, 166.
  See also instructional
  formats
states, transfer courses within,
  134–135
state-supported college information
  websites, 254–258
statistics, 122
STEM (Science, Technology,
  Engineering and Math)
  core course requirements in, 86
  prerequisites in, 91
  university game plans and, 187
stories of students. *See* case studies
strategy for university studies. *See*
  GPAMaxx Strategy
strengths and weaknesses
  case studies of, 242
  determining, 159–163
  introduction to, 153–154

stringent grading, 89
student evaluations, 180–181
student examples. *See* case studies
student loans, 3, 5
study guides, 126
summa cum laude, 63
switching majors, 93

T
time of day, 156
time-intensive requirements, 92
timely graduation
  cost of education and, 21–22
  credit by examination for, 113,
    120
  credit hours and, 35
  grade replacement policies and,
    43
  statistics on, 2, 15–16
  strategies for, generally, 17
  transfer courses for, 142
timing of exams for credit, 128
transfer courses
  action plans for, 204–205
  advantages of, 137–143
  on-campus courses vs., 133–134
  case studies of, 241
  CBE vs., 144
  in Course Selection Module,
    216–218, 224, 234, 241
  cumulative GPAs and, 145–146
  difficult degree requirements
    via, 137–138, 141–142
  dual enrollment for, 135–137
  early graduation via, 137, 142
  example of, 139–143, 146–148
  high school courses qualifying
    as, 135–137
  institutional GPAs and, 137–138,
    141–142, 145
  introduction to, 99, 133
  lighter course loads via, 138, 142
  pitfalls of, 143–148
  prioritizing enrollment via, 143

transfer courses (*continued*)
　priority for course registration
　　via, 138–139, 142–143
　resources on, 250–254
　rules/policies governing, 84,
　　134–135
　in same state, 134–135
　saving money via, 142
　strategic selection of, 143–144
　timely graduation via, 137, 142
　in university game plans,
　　193–194, 204–205
transition to college, 6–8, 10–11,
　89
two-year colleges, 15, 140–141,
　145–148, 195

U
Udacity, 127
unhappiness in college, 46
United Kingdom, 110

university grading practices. *See*
　grading practices
university master game plans
　development of, 206–207
　evolution of, 208
　introduction to, 19, 191
University of Florida, 50–51
University of Virginia, 22
university road maps. *See* degree plans
university-specific exams, 109
upper-division courses, 91, 112

W
weaknesses
　case studies of, 234, 242
　credit by examination for, 130–131
　determining, 159–163
　introduction to, 153–154
weed-out courses, 58, 139–140
withdrawing from classes, 181–182
workloads, 157

About GPAMaxx®

GPAMaxx® is an education startup with a groundbreaking approach to academic advising. With our launch in 2015, we're pioneering an innovative, achievement-oriented advising service for public-university-bound students. To learn more about GPAMaxx, please visit us at www.GPAMaxx.com.

About the Author

Jeff Gimpel is the founder of GPAMaxx® and an attorney. A Phi Beta Kappa and high honors graduate of the University of Texas at Austin, Jeff earned his bachelor's degree in three years. Although he graduated early, he completed a double major in German and history as well as the Liberal Arts Honors Program. Jeff also holds a law degree with honors from the University of Texas School of Law, and a master's degree in German law from the Ludwig-Maximilians University in Munich, Germany, where he studied as a Fulbright Scholar. Prior to founding GPAMaxx, Jeff practiced corporate law for more than a decade in New York and Hong Kong with the international law firm Clifford Chance.

He can be reached at Jeff@GPAMaxx.com.